JULIE LEFEBURE

# RIGHT NOW MATTERS

## BIBLE STUDY

A 28-Day Guided Adventure
to Living as a Right-Now Woman

Cover & interior design by Typewriter Creative Co.

Unless otherwise noted, Scripture quotations are from THE HOLY BIBLE, NEW INTERNATIONAL VERSION®, NIV® Copyright © 1973, 1978, 1984, 2011 by Biblica, Inc.® Used by permission. All rights reserved worldwide.

Scripture quotations marked Voice are taken from The Voice™. Copyright © 2008 by Ecclesia Bible Society. Used by permission. All rights reserved.

Scripture quotations marked MSG are taken from THE MESSAGE, copyright © 1993, 2002, 2018 by Eugene H. Peterson. Used by permission of NavPress. All rights reserved. Represented by Tyndale House Publishers, Inc.

Scripture quotations marked NLT are taken from the Holy Bible, New Living Translation, copyright © 1996, 2004, 2015 by Tyndale House Foundation. Used by permission of Tyndale House Publishers, Inc., Carol Stream, Illinois 60188. All rights reserved.

Scripture quotations market TLB are taken from The Living Bible, copyright © 1971 by Tyndale House Foundation. Used by permission of Tyndale House Publishers Inc., Carol Stream, Illinois 60188. All rights reserved.

ISBN 979-8-9890693-2-3 (Paperback)
ISBN 979-8-9890693-3-0 (eBook)

# Contents

# Introduction

Living undistracted: is it even achievable in this culture of distraction?

It's no secret that distractions are everywhere—in our homes and workplaces, in our social media feeds, through our devices in our pockets, purses, and hands, even in our own thoughts. How can we possibly overcome them all? *Is it possible?*

Years ago, when I first began this quest to pursue an undistracted life, no one was talking about it. No one was discussing distractions and how they were impacting our lives. Nowhere could I find practical and tangible resources on the matter to help and guide me with next steps. Consequently, at times I thought I was crazy or losing my mind, and I certainly felt alone. *Am I the only one so distracted? Why is no one discussing this?* Then I began talking about *my* distractions. Ah! I soon found other women could relate.

Stories then began to surface of women who, like me, were missing the priceless moments of life happening right in front of them—like the woman who was so focused on excelling in her job, she missed most of her children's after-school activities, only to realize later how important those were. Or like the teenager who looked up from her phone and for the first time understood she was more concerned with her online world than her real-life world. Then there was the young mom who was so distracted by her regrets of the past she couldn't embrace her beautiful life right now.

Distractions were robbing these women of their peace and joy, not to mention God's blessings and gifts of the present moment. I saw their grimaced faces as they shyly shared their experiences, and I felt the heaviness of their heartaches as they recalled moments they missed and could never get back. From my own personal experiences, I fully understood their pain.

Sound familiar? Can you relate to these women, too? Are distractions robbing you of God's gift of the present moment?

Right now matters.

I knew there had to be a better—and more fulfilling—way to live. After all, Jesus came to give us a life of abundance, right? At least that's what it says in the Bible: "The thief approaches *with malicious intent,* looking to steal, slaughter, and destroy; I came to give life with joy and abundance" (John 10:10 Voice).

Yet our everyday distractions are robbing us of that abundant, joy-filled life. Not only this, but they are negatively impacting our moods, our relationships, our sleep, and our everyday realities. They even affect our faith and our relationship with God. Distractions are far more serious than we realize. We can either continue to give in to these distractions, or we can choose to claim this abundant life as our own. The choice is up to us.

Right now matters.

There's got to be more to life than this! And friend, there is.

Throughout the Bible, God demonstrates His plan for us to live in the moment and to embrace right now—not to be concerned about the past or the future, but to meet Him in the present. He guides us throughout Scripture to seek the things that are important and to forget the things that aren't. His Word leads us along pathways that are His best for us, and He promises He'll walk with us every step of the way.

This undistracted life *is* possible. How? Because God and His plans for our lives are bigger—and better—than the distractions we face. We have hope because God won't leave us in this distracted mess when we turn to Him for help. Plus, we have a perfect example to follow of One who lived an undistracted life, documented in the pages of Scripture—Jesus.

I often refer to this life as an "adventure with God." Embracing a right-now life and intentionally living in the moment is an exhilarating adventure as we partner with the Lord. It's one full of exciting possibilities and never-before-experienced opportunities. It contains unique joys and generous memory-making moments. As God leads us to new places and new heights in this adventure, He molds us into the women He desires us to be—the women He created us to be. We become changed. We become what I term "Right-Now Women."

These are women who understand the importance of living undistracted and staying fully present. They choose to live in the right-now moment, even if they may do it imperfectly. They embrace the abundant life Jesus came to give them, and they understand that living this way is for their growth, for the good of others, and for God's glory.

Living undistracted is countercultural. It's against the norm. But you know as well as I do, the norm isn't always God's way. Choosing to live in a different manner with different choices isn't easy. But who said living an abundant life would ever be easy? Jesus certainly didn't. It will take time to learn this new way of living, and we might feel like giving up every now and then. But if we keep putting one foot in front of the other, keeping our focus on Jesus, a life of peace and joy will be ours.

Right now matters.

Look at you in this moment! You picked up this study and are reading these words. You took the first brave step in embracing this new way of living. I am so proud of you. I am praying for you. God and I will be with you every step through this adventure.

Whether you walk through this study solo or with a group of friends, my prayer is that you will experience what Jesus described in Matthew 11:28-30 when He said, "'Are you tired? Worn out? Burned out on religion? Come to me. Get away with me and you'll recover your life. I'll show you how to take a real rest. Walk with me and work with me—watch how I do it. Learn the unforced rhythms of grace. I won't lay anything heavy or ill-fitting on you. Keep company with me and you'll learn to live freely and lightly'" (MSG).

It's time to live freely and lightly, friend. It is possible. Let's embark on this adventure together.

# How to Benefit the Most from This Study

This is a guidebook of sorts for the Right-Now Woman. It's your personal tool for learning, step-by-step, how to recognize distractions and release them from your life. It's a study guide to take you deeper into God's Word as you search Scriptures and learn what God has to say. It's also a journal where you can openly share your thoughts, your "aha!" moments, your prayers, and whatever else is on your heart. Each day you'll be invited to go deeper within yourself and with God. Don't be afraid to open yourself up a little. God can use this for your growth and freedom. You and God are the only two who will see what you've written, so feel free to be open and honest with both of you.

Allow this book to be your friend and companion for the next twenty-eight days.

Regarding that, I encourage you to give yourself grace. You live a real life, and you might not be able to open this book and spend the time in it that you'd like for twenty-eight days in a row. I get it, and that's okay. Sure, I always suggest spending time in God's Word every day, but please don't get discouraged or frustrated if you miss a day (or two or three) of this book. When you are able to return, simply pick back up where you left off. No one or nothing says you must complete this in twenty-eight days in a row.

Just take it one day at a time.

## WITH THIS BOOK, YOU WILL NEED A PENCIL OR PEN, ALONG WITH THE FOLLOWING:

1.  A desire to grow in your faith and learn from God. As with any other area in life, when we want to make a change or grow, we need to be intentional. The same goes for this study. We can either skim through it and quickly cross it off our list for the day, or we can take our time and allow God to teach us, mold us, and transform us through it. The

choice is ours. We will get out of it what we put in. Some suggestions for your study:

- carve out time in your daily schedule for your study (I suggest 20-30 minutes)
- prepare your heart beforehand by asking the Holy Spirit to enlighten your mind and teach you
- remove as many distractions in your environment as you can
- refuse to rush through your study
- prayerfully consider each question and prompt
- be authentic and honest with God and yourself
- embrace the truths God teaches you
- apply what you're learning to your current life and circumstances

2.   A Bible. Unless otherwise indicated, I quote from the New International Version in this study. You may use this version or another version of choice. You can also access a Bible online through websites such as biblehub.com, blueletterbible.com, or biblegateway.com, or through an app on your phone.

3.   My book *Right Now Matters: Empowering Right-Now Women in a Culture of Distraction.* Having access to the book will help you, as it is the foundation of this study. We will expand on the concepts and ideas of the book through each session, and it will aid you in understanding the backstories and the direction we're headed. *Right Now Matters* is not required, but it will positively impact your study since many questions correlate with the content of the book.

## WHAT YOU'LL FIND IN EACH DAY'S STUDY:

Each chapter in *Right Now Matters* is represented by two days in this study, except for Days 1 and 2, which reference both the Introduction and Chapter 1 of *Right Now Matters.* For example, Days 3 and 4 pertain to Chapter 2 of *Right Now Matters,* and Days 5 and 6 pertain to Chapter 3.

I'll emphasize this again. Give yourself some grace and take the pressure off. Take your time and enjoy this study at your pace. This study doesn't exist to add stress to your life—but to remove it. So don't let our spiritual enemy trick you into believing if you don't finish this in twenty-eight days that you have failed. That's a lie. Any progress you make in this book is progress. Celebrate that.

Each day contains the same components in the form of an acrostic for RIGHT NOW:

**R**    Ready    (ready and prepare your heart)
**I**    Inquire (inquire within)
**G**    Give    (give yourself permission)
**H**    Heart    (the heart of the lesson)
**T**    Truth    (read truth of the Bible)
**N**    New    (new thoughts, ideas, lessons)
**O**    Open    (open yourself to something different)
**W**    Walk    (walk in what you're learning)

You'll be led through each day's content and will be encouraged to apply it to your life. These prompts will simplify the process and aid you in living as a Right-Now Woman.

As I share in the Introduction of *Right Now Matters,* distractions interrupt our lives and pull us away from living in the present, from staying in the *right now.* And the thing is, right now is what each of us has in our possession. Right now is the most important moment because it's the one we're currently living. Not yesterday and not tomorrow. All we have is right now. Right now matters.

Are you ready to grow in your faith in God, to dig deep in Scripture, and to be equipped to live the abundant life Jesus came to give you? Turn the page, and we'll begin our adventure together. I'm glad I get to journey with you.

# DAY 1

*Right-Now Women are willing to step
out of what's comfortable.*

---

## READY

Take a slow, deep breath. Prepare your heart. Ask the Holy Spirit to enlighten your mind, remove distractions, and open your heart to what God has for you today.

Pray:

*Lord, as I begin this journey of learning how to live undistracted and remain in the moment, I come before You with open hands and an open heart. I am grateful You have drawn me to this study and are taking me deeper in my faith walk with You. Enlighten my mind through the power of the Holy Spirit, remove any distractions that could hinder my time with You, and teach me what You desire for me to learn today. Amen.*

Today and tomorrow, read the Introduction and Chapter 1 of *Right Now Matters*.

## INQUIRE

Why did you decide to take this Right Now Matters adventure through this study? What do you hope to learn or gain through it? Write down your answers here.

_____

_____

---

---

---

What has caused you to live distracted lately? Write all the distractions that come to mind. We will return to this list on Day 7.

---

---

---

---

---

## GIVE

Give yourself permission to dig a little deeper. After reading my story of missing my son's goal in the Introduction of *Right Now Matters,* ponder your own experiences. Think of a time when you missed something important—a moment you'll never get back—because of distractions. Write it here.

---

---

---

---

---

After reliving this experience in your mind, how does it make you feel? What emotions arise within you?

_____

_____

_____

_____

_____

_____

_____

_____

Allow any emotions to motivate you to dig deeper in this study. Give yourself permission to take the necessary steps to learn all you can how to live undistracted so you never experience a moment like that again.

## HEART

Before we move on, release any guilt or shame regarding the past mistakes you've made in living undistracted. It's wise to ask God for forgiveness and anyone else that God brings to your mind regarding these past mistakes.

Right or wrong, for years I didn't share with my son, Zach, that I missed his goal. In fact, he really didn't know until I asked him to read the Introduction of _Right Now Matters._ I had already asked God to forgive me, but after Zach read the story, I asked him to forgive me, too. When we release these past mistakes into God's hands, we can walk in the freedom of His grace and forgiveness.

Be open with God, and write out what you want to say to Him—whether it's a prayer, some thoughts, or words in your heart. Spend these moments in silence with Him.

_____

_____

_____

_____

_____

## TRUTH

God's Word is filled with truths regarding forgiveness and grace. Open your Bible and locate the references below. I encourage you to write out the passages or add any notes beside each one. You may want to return to these later.

1 John 1:9

_____

_____

_____

Matthew 6:14-15

_____

_____

_____

_____

Psalm 103:12

_____

_____

_____

_____

Psalm 86:5

_____

_____

_____

_____

Think through these Scriptures. How can you apply one of them to your life today?

_____

_____

_____

_____

_____

## NEW

Distracted living occurs anytime something causes us to shift our focus from the present. What new thought is God giving you about living distracted in the past, forgiving yourself for that, and living differently in the future?

Write it out here.

_____

_____

_____

_____

_____

## OPEN

Write a letter to yourself as you begin this journey. It can include forgiving yourself for how you've lived distracted in the past, for how you intend to live from this day forward, or anything you want yourself to remember about right now.

Dear

_____

_____

_____

_____

_____

_____

_____

_____

_____

_____

_____

_____

Love,

## WALK

**Right-Now Women are willing to step out of what's comfortable.** You're doing this by completing Day 1. Congratulations! Now it's time to walk it out.

Write down what you learned today, what you intend to apply to your life, and how you plan to commit to living undistracted.

_____

_____

_____

_____

Well done, Right-Now Woman!

Pray:

_Thank You, God, for teaching me today, for opening my eyes and heart to Your truth, and for helping me learn how I can make changes to live the undistracted life You desire for me. I trust You in this journey, one day at a time. Amen._

Use the space on the next page to journal any additional prayers, thoughts, or insights.

# DAY 2

*Right-Now Women make the most of right now.*

## READY

Take a slow, deep breath. Prepare your heart. Ask the Holy Spirit to enlighten your mind, remove distractions, and open your heart to what God has for you today.

Pray:

*Lord, thank You for this time with You. I come with my hands and heart open to what You have for me. Please remove any distractions during this time so I can wholeheartedly focus on You. Through the influence of the Holy Spirit, give me eyes to see and a mind to understand and apply what You teach me. Draw me closer to You in these moments. Amen.*

Continue reading the Introduction and Chapter 1 of *Right Now Matters*.

## INQUIRE

After reading the story of my husband's biking accident in Chapter 1 of *Right Now Matters,* did you follow the prompt to think about what is important to you? How do you answer that question today? Write down your answer.

_____

_____

_____

_____

What prevents you from seeing this moment as the gift it is? Circle all that apply to you or your situation:

| | |
|---|---|
| busyness | worry |
| boredom | difficulties |
| discouragement | unhappiness |
| disinterest | stress |
| apathy | discontentment |
| overcommitment | hurry |
| restlessness | trauma |
| interruptions | other people |
| agitations | |

Or write others here:

_____

_____

_____

_____

Are you surprised by any of your answers? If so, which one(s)?

_____

_____

_____

_____

_____

Can you trust God with your answers? If so, how will you do that today?

_____

_____

_____

_____

_____

_____

_____

## GIVE

Give yourself permission to examine your perception of this moment and embrace new thoughts and ideas regarding it.

## HEART

Right now matters. It's where God is and where He desires to meet us. It's the only moment God is present with us. Whether it's a monumental and memorable moment or one that goes unnoticed, this moment matters. Why? Because God created it.

Understandably, Bill's biking accident woke me up to the gift of each moment and to the gift of him in my life. I realized I had begun to take him for granted. We don't intend to, but sometimes we do this with whatever—or whoever—is closest to us. I was guilty of that, and maybe you are realizing the same in your relationships right now. Thankfully, it's not too late to appreciate each moment God gives us, and it's not too late to appreciate those special people who God has gifted us. May right now be a fresh start and a new beginning to live differently.

Before we move on, take a few minutes to thank God for this very moment—even if it feels mundane or ordinary. Be open with God and write out everything that's on your heart right now.

_____

_____

_____

_____

_____

## TRUTH

This moment isn't coincidental or random. God knew when He created you that you would be here right now reading these words. He's with us in the moments He created! To drive this home a little further, let's look at the first days of creation in Scripture. Open your Bible and read the creation account in Genesis 1:1-2:3.

What did God create on each day?

Day 1: _____

Day 2: _____

Day 3: _____

Day 4: _____

Day 5: _____

Day 6: _____

Day 7: _____

If you answered "nothing" or something similar on Day 7, you're right. What did God do on Day 7 instead? Why?

_____

_____

_____

_____

_____

Which day of creation stands out to you the most? Why?

_____

_____

_____

_____

_____

Five Bible verses referencing the word "now" are listed on pages 18 and 19 in Chapter 1 of *Right Now Matters.* In the space below, write down the one verse that speaks to you or intrigues you the most regarding your current circumstances.

_____

_____

_____

_____

_____

## NEW

All we have is right now, and we don't get another opportunity to live this moment. What new thought or truth is God revealing to you today, either through the Bible verses or the questions? Write it down here.

_____

_____

_____

_____

_____

_____

## OPEN

List the most important people in your life at this moment.

1. _____

2. _____

3. _____

4. _____

5. _____

6. _____

7. _____

8. _____

9. _____

10. _____

Take time today to tell them how important they are to you—even if you think they already know. Send a text. Write an email. Make a phone call. Meet for coffee. Mail a card. Don't wait until a more convenient or opportune time. Right now is the perfect time to appreciate these priceless gifts in your life.

## WALK

**Right-Now Women make the most of right now.** They don't live it out perfectly, nor do they try to. They simply embrace this moment and determine to live each one God gives them to the fullest. Good job on completing Day 2. Now it's time to walk it out.

Write down what you learned today, what you intend to apply to your life, and how you plan to commit to making the most of each moment.

_____

_____

_____

_____

_____

_____

_____

Well done, Right-Now Woman!

Pray:

*Thank You, God, for guiding my thoughts and my will to Your truth today and for teaching me the value and importance of this moment and this day. I now realize this moment matters because You created it. Help me to live in each moment and embrace each day from here forward. Amen.*

Use the space on the next page to journal any additional prayers, thoughts, or insights.

# DAY 3

*Right-Now Women focus on living abundant lives.*

---

## READY

Take a slow, deep breath. Prepare your heart. Ask the Holy Spirit to enlighten your mind, remove distractions, and open your heart to what God has for you today.

Pray:

*Lord, thank You for this day and for this time with You. I open my heart to what You have for me today. Please remove any distractions now so I can completely focus on You. Holy Spirit, enlighten my mind to be able to understand what You want me to learn, and give me Your wisdom to apply it. Draw me closer to You during this time. Amen.*

Today and tomorrow, read Chapter 2 of *Right Now Matters.*

## INQUIRE

After reading my *there's-got-to-be-more-to-life-than-this* story in Chapter 2 of *Right Now Matters,* does this resonate with you? Have you ever felt like there's got to be more to life than this, or do you feel this way now? Write down your thoughts and why you felt—or might be feeling—this way.

_____

_____

_____

_____

## GIVE

Give yourself permission to explore any feelings of *there's got to be more to life than this.* Sometimes we try to ignore them or attempt to brush them aside. If you're feeling this way or have in the past, it's for a reason. God may be trying to get your attention, like He did with me.

## HEART

Distractions often draw us away from God's good plans and purposes for our lives. They are sneaky, and they often affect us a little at a time until we find ourselves completely off course. Our spiritual enemy is behind many of these distractions, enticing us into living unproductive and ineffective lives. He recognizes what will keep us from becoming the women God desires us to be.

For years this enemy distracted me from writing the book that was on my heart—the book that I knew God was nudging me to write: *Right Now Matters.* The things he distracted me with weren't necessarily "bad" things, but they kept me from doing what God was calling me to do—things such as scrolling through social media, or fun but not fulfilling activities, or even putting off what was important until I "felt" like doing it. These took my attention away from the better things God wanted me to pursue, and they kept me unproductive and ineffective.

Before we move on, think about this: could this spiritual enemy be using distractions to keep you unproductive and ineffective? Write down anything God may be revealing to you right now.

_____

_____

_____

_____

_____

_____

## TRUTH

In Chapter 2 of *Right Now Matters* we ponder John 10:10 and how this thief comes to steal, kill, and destroy, and the hope we have in the abundant life Jesus came to give us. Now let's peer into the full context of what Jesus was saying in this passage. Open your Bible, and read John 10:1-10. Write down any words or phrases that stand out to you.

_____

_____

_____

_____

_____

_____

Jesus explains in verse 4 how the sheep follow the gatekeeper because they are familiar with his voice. They wouldn't follow a stranger.

This reminds me of our three farm cats who live on our land. They were born here, so I know these cats and they know me. They are adults now, and I'm the one who feeds them, talks to them, and cares for them daily. I also make sure they have shelter when the harsh Iowa winters blow in. They know my voice. It's interesting that when they see me, they'll still often scatter. That is, until I speak to them—then they come running my way. They don't know my husband's voice, however. When he talks, they flee. They will follow me, but they won't follow him.

The only way we get to know Jesus' voice is by spending time with Him. This happens by learning His ways and hearing His voice through Scripture. But if we aren't familiar with His voice (not necessarily His audible voice), we will follow other voices we hear—like a stranger's, or the world's, or even the voice of our spiritual enemy.

What are some ways you can spend time with Jesus to get to know His voice? (Some ideas: read your Bible, pray, listen to worship songs, praise Him, sit with Him in quiet spaces, write a letter to Him.) Write down your ideas.

_____

_____

_____

_____

_____

_____

## NEW

Distractions aren't just something to avoid to make our lives more enjoyable, they are something to avoid to make our lives more impactful. What new revelation is God showing you regarding living an impactful life or about listening for Jesus' voice? Write it out here.

_____

_____

_____

_____

_____

## OPEN

Just for fun, find inspiring words regarding living an impactful life in the word search below. If you don't have time to do this activity right now, feel free to return to it later. (Answer key is on page 235.)

| A | S | F | R | I | E | N | D | S | E | T | R | O | X | P |
|---|---|---|---|---|---|---|---|---|---|---|---|---|---|---|
| E | L | A | S | T | I | N | G | A | U | C | Z | V | Q | L |
| P | G | E | H | H | K | N | W | V | D | S | A | E | A | G |
| O | B | K | R | T | G | R | D | O | U | X | E | R | Q | E |
| H | E | A | R | T | Y | U | G | R | N | B | V | J | G | N |
| B | N | W | M | O | W | E | A | Q | D | A | X | O | C | C |
| X | L | A | P | G | L | V | P | L | I | V | E | Y | V | O |
| Z | Y | E | N | U | F | O | C | U | S | B | N | E | M | U |
| G | N | I | S | S | E | L | B | T | T | C | F | D | T | R |
| Y | I | T | N | E | S | E | R | P | R | U | A | I | C | A |
| T | D | F | G | H | J | L | A | K | A | O | M | P | A | G |
| O | F | S | T | I | M | E | V | J | C | H | I | N | P | E |
| D | E | V | B | M | O | M | E | N | T | E | L | I | M | S |
| A | T | R | I | N | S | P | I | R | E | I | Y | P | I | L |
| Y | Q | D | S | A | A | B | U | N | D | A | N | T | J | K |

| | | | | |
|---|---|---|---|---|
| ABUNDANT | ENCOURAGE | GIFT | IMPACT | LAUGH |
| OPEN | TODAY | ALERT | FAMILY | GOD |
| INSPIRE | LIVE | TIME | SMILE | OVERJOYED |
| AWAKE | FOCUS | GRACE | JESUS | LOVE |
| PRESENT | UNDISTRACTED | BLESSING | FRIENDS | HEART |
| MOMENT | SAVOR | BRAVE | FUN | HOPE |
| LASTING | NOW | | | |

## WALK

**Right-Now Women focus on living abundant lives.** Great job completing Day 3. It's time to walk it out.

Write down what you learned today, what you intend to apply to your life, and how you will address any *there's-got-to-be-more-to-life-than-this* feelings or thoughts.

_____

_____

_____

_____

_____

Well done, Right-Now Woman!

Pray:

*God, thank You for helping me understand how there is likely more behind the distractions that lure me away from You than I realize. You're opening my eyes to see that distractions aren't just something to avoid to make my life more enjoyable, they are something to avoid to make my life more impactful. Continue to help me see Your truth. Amen.*

Use the space on the next page to journal any additional prayers, thoughts, or insights.

# DAY 4

*Right-Now Women focus on living in the moment.*

## READY

Take a slow, deep breath. Prepare your heart. Ask the Holy Spirit to enlighten your mind, remove distractions, and open your heart to what God has for you today.

Pray:

*Lord, I praise You for what You are teaching me already in this study and I look forward to this time with You today. Guide my thoughts and my focus to You and Your will. Please remove any distraction that tries to entice me away during this time. Holy Spirit, equip me to understand and embrace truth today. Amen.*

Continue reading Chapter 2 of *Right Now Matters.*

## INQUIRE

When we live distracted, we miss what's important in life. Think for a few moments and ask yourself, what have you been missing in your life lately? Oftentimes we don't know until we begin to pay attention. Ponder that as we move deeper into today's study. Write down what comes to mind.

_____

_____

_____

_____

## GIVE

Give yourself permission to pause to examine just how distracted you have been lately. Read through the indications on pages 34-36 in Chapter 2 of *Right Now Matters.* Do any of these describe you? If so, which ones?

_____

_____

_____

_____

_____

_____

_____

It may not feel comfortable to face reality, but doing so always opens us up to healing and wholeness. This is a good and blessed thing!

## HEART

Distracted living negatively impacts our quality of life. We can't focus when we're distracted, nor can we follow our purpose or the direction we know to take. Distractions can have such a hold on us that we may not even realize their magnitude.

We just go through the motions, day after day, week after week, month after month. Pretty soon these months turn into years, and we look back one day and question where the time has gone. Will we get to the end of our lives and wonder the same? Will we regret that we didn't fully live the lives God gave us? Oh, friend, I pray this won't be the case.

There's got to be more to life than this. There is. And we're going to find it.

Write down anything God may be revealing to you right now.

_____

_____

_____

_____

_____

_____

## TRUTH

Mary found out what was more important in her life. Open your Bible to Luke 10:38-42. Read this account of the sisters Mary and Martha with Jesus. Even if it may be familiar to you, 1 invite you to see this passage through fresh eyes. Read it slowly and intentionally.

What stands out to you the most in this passage? Why?

_____

_____

_____

_____

_____

Which sister do you resemble? Are you more like Martha or more like Mary? If Jesus came to your home today, would you sit at His feet, like Mary, or do you think you'd be making everything perfect for His visit, like Martha?

Share your answers here.

_____

_____

_____

_____

_____

I disclose in *Right Now Matters* that I desire to be more like Mary, but I believe I'm more like Martha. That's probably true daily. It's not that I don't want to sit at Jesus' feet, but goodness, there's so much to prepare and do! Mary, however, displayed for us what was most important: sitting with Jesus, learning from Him, and spending time with Him. She wasn't going through the motions of life. She wasn't preoccupied or distracted. She was living in the moment, soaking up everything Jesus had for her. The preparations and dinner could wait. This moment with Jesus would not. I want to be more like Mary. Do you, too?

## NEW

Mary found the answer to *there's got to be more to life than this.* What does this mean for you? What new idea or thought is God presenting to you about living undistracted like Mary? Write it down here.

_____

_____

_____

_____

_____

## OPEN

Distractions keep us stuck. They keep us miserable, and they certainly don't lead us to find the answer to *there's got to be more to life than this.* It's time to dream a little. Maybe it's been a while since you've done so, and maybe you think it's too late to dream again. You had dreams as a little girl. Some you may be living today, and some got buried under the responsibilities, demands, reality, and distractions of life. What's your dream? You have one. Ask God to reveal it to you. Write it in a cloud below, along with others that surface in your heart and mind.

## WALK

**Right-Now Women focus on living in the moment.** They stay present and refuse to miss what truly matters for what's less important. Great job completing Day 4. It's time to walk it out.

Right now matters. Write down what you learned today, what you intend to apply to your life, and how you will take one step toward a dream you dreamt of today.

_____

_____

_____

_____

_____

Well done, Right-Now Woman!

Pray:

_God, thank You for helping me see how distractions have overtaken me. Thank You for helping me understand there is more to life than this. I can live in the moment and dream again because of You. Help me to walk this out in real life. I need You. Amen._

Use the space on the next page to journal any additional prayers, thoughts, or insights.

# DAY 5

*Right-Now Women understand living too*
*busy causes us to live distracted.*

---

## READY

Take a slow, deep breath. Prepare your heart. Ask the Holy Spirit to enlighten your mind, remove distractions, and open your heart to what God has for you today.

Pray:

*I praise and thank You, God, for these moments with You. Please quiet my mind and heart, and open them to the truth You desire to teach me today. Guard me against any distractions that try to interrupt our time together. Holy Spirit, help me to receive and understand what You want me to learn, and help me apply it to my life. Amen.*

Today and tomorrow, read Chapter 3 of *Right Now Matters*.

## INQUIRE

God uses sunrises to refresh and refocus me. I share that life-changing sunrise morning in Chapter 3 of *Right Now Matters*. What does God use to refresh and refocus you? If you're not sure, pay attention to what causes you to pause and take a second look. Notice what makes your heart feel all warm and fuzzy. Write it down here or come back later after God shows you.

_____

_____

_____

_____

_____

## GIVE

Give yourself permission to step back from "busy," and welcome differing thoughts about busyness in your life. Have you previously considered being busy a badge of honor? Do you believe the busier you are, the more important you are? Explore your ideas about busyness, and write down what comes to mind here.

_____

_____

_____

_____

_____

## HEART

Are we missing out on life because we're too busy to notice? Living too busy causes us to live distracted. What if, today, we halted all this busyness and chose to intentionally slow things down—our thinking, our driving, our talking, our walking. What if we walked our errands instead of running them? And what if we decided to jump off the spinning-out-of-control hamster wheel before we hurt ourselves or someone else?

Not long ago I was pushing the grocery cart up and down the aisles, scanning my grocery list, and crossing items off as I put them in my cart. I was on a mission to get in and out of the store as fast as possible. After all, I had places to go and people to see.

As I was nearing the end of my list, I heard someone say, "Hi, Julie." I turned around and saw an acquaintance from long ago. When I get focused, I tend to not notice anything else around me, and this was also true in the grocery store. I didn't see her—and wouldn't have—if she didn't say hello to me.

I pushed my list aside as we chatted in aisle three. She was more important than my groceries, and our conversation was uplifting and life-giving to both of us. I'm guessing God slowed me down for a reason—or multiple reasons—that day. I'm thankful He did.

## TRUTH

Busyness is not God's best for us, and Jesus is a perfect example of this. Can you recall any account in the Bible where we see Jesus distracted with busyness? Let's peer into two passages of Scripture. Open your Bible, and read the references below.

John 11:1-15

How many days did Jesus stay where He was after learning of Lazarus' illness?

_____

_____

Why do you think He stayed there instead of hurrying to Lazarus' side?

_____

_____

_____

_____

_____

What can you learn from Jesus regarding busyness?

_____

_____

_____

_____

_____

Matthew 12:14-15

Even though Jesus knew the Pharisees were plotting to kill Him, what did He do after withdrawing from that area?

_____

_____

_____

_____

Would that be your focus and mine, or would our focus be more about preserving our own lives?

_____

_____

_____

_____

What's one thing you can apply to your life from Jesus' example?

_____

_____

_____

_____

_____

Sure, Jesus had important things to do, but He was never distracted by busyness. He healed the sick, He taught the crowds, He fed the hungry, and He ministered to the multitudes. But He was never too busy. We can glean much from His example today.

## NEW

Living too busy causes us to live distracted. What new thought is God guiding you to regarding busyness and the pace of your life? Write it out here.

_____

_____

_____

_____

_____

## OPEN

So often our pace determines our peace. On the next page are some tangible ways to "slow your go." Put an asterisk next to the ones that make sense and seem reasonable to you.

_____ Use the crock pot instead of the microwave.

_____ Choose to walk and not run.

_____ Intentionally slow down in the grocery or department store, and notice the people around you. Maybe even offer a smile.

_____ Savor your food while you eat instead of rushing through dinner.

_____ Take your time getting ready in the morning (you may need to add an extra fifteen minutes to your morning routine).

_____ Drive the speed limit—the real speed limit, not five over.

_____ Refuse to tell your children or grandchildren to "hurry up."

_____ Sit for five minutes sporadically throughout your day to breathe deeply.

_____ Send a note to someone through postal mail instead of a text or email.

_____ Take a nap.

_____ Take a real lunch break, and refuse to work through it.

_____ When life feels as if it's spinning out of control, lift your eyes and ask God for His help.

What other ideas did these generate for you? Write them down here.

_____

_____

_____

_____

_____

## WALK

**Right-Now Women understand living too busy causes us to live distracted.** Congratulations on completing Day 5. It's time to walk it out.

Write down what you learned today, what you intend to apply to your life, and how you will begin to look at busyness differently.

_____

_____

_____

_____

_____

Well done, Right-Now Woman!

Pray:

*Thank You, God, for showing me how busy is not Your best for me. Living in this bustling world, I've become accustomed to a fast-paced lifestyle. I know that's not necessarily a bad thing, but when it's distracting me from the life You've blessed me with, it's a problem. Help me to live at a pace that glorifies You, and remind me of this if I slide back into my old ways of busy. Thank You for guiding me. Amen.*

Use the space on the next page to journal any additional prayers, thoughts, or insights.

# DAY 6

*Right-Now Women remove busy from our lives.*

---

## READY

Take a slow, deep breath. Prepare your heart. Ask the Holy Spirit to enlighten your mind, remove distractions, and open your heart to what God has for you today.

Pray:

*Lord, thank You for this time with You. You are never too busy for me. May I never be too busy for You! I come to You today with an excited expectation to learn and grow in Your presence. Remove any distractions that try to interrupt this time with You. Holy Spirit, please open my mind and heart to receive all You have for me today. Thank You. Amen.*

Continue reading Chapter 3 of *Right Now Matters*.

## INQUIRE

How often do you use the word "busy" to describe yourself or your life? If someone asks you how you are, how do you respond? Do you ever say you're "so busy"? Think about this for a few minutes, and write down anything that comes to mind.

_____

_____

_____

_____

## GIVE

Give yourself permission to remove busy from your life and your vocabulary. Much of how we live begins in our thoughts and our words. This matters.

## HEART

How many times in a day or a week do we say the words "I'm busy"? We may not even realize we say it because it's such a common response. Recently our two-year-old grandson surprisingly asked his Papa and me, "How was your day?" We both smiled and replied that our days were good. Then we asked him about his day. He replied, "It was busy." Oh goodness. Don't tell me this now begins at two years old?

As I mention in Chapter 3 of *Right Now Matters,* one practical and powerful way to halt the busyness in our lives is to remove the word "busy" from our vocabularies. It may sound too silly and simple to be impactful, but trust me—this works. I invite you to try this today. Do all you can to not let the word "busy" escape from your lips. Then do it again tomorrow, then the next day, and the next day. Just one day at a time. I believe you'll be amazed by what a difference this makes in your life!

## TRUTH

As with any new habit we form, it takes time, intention, and dedicated effort. Oftentimes we don't build a new habit easily because it may be a one-step-forward, two-steps-back kind of progress. But if we keep at this—removing busy from our lives and our vocabularies—we'll find a more peaceful and less stressful life. We may need some encouragement along the way, however.

On the next page are four Bible verses to spur us on as we build this new habit of releasing busyness. We can read and meditate on them when we find ourselves reverting back to our ways of entertaining a busy and hectic lifestyle. They are perfect for whenever we get discouraged or need hope from God's Word. Open your Bible, read them, and write them out. You may want to refer to them later, too.

Matthew 11:28-30

_____

_____

_____

_____

_____

_____

Proverbs 3:5-6

_____

_____

_____

_____

_____

John 14:27

_____

_____

_____

_____

_____

Isaiah 41:10

_____

_____

_____

_____

## NEW

Busyness not only invades our lives, it also permeates our language. What new insight is God showing you regarding the busyness of your life or how often you say the word "busy"? Write it out here.

_____

_____

_____

_____

_____

_____

_____

_____

_____

_____

## OPEN

In Chapter 3 of *Right Now Matters,* 1 share how 1 replaced the word "busy" with "full." Let's think of some other words that we can say instead of "busy." Brainstorm with me and circle any that stand out to you.

PEPPY                EFFECTIVE                ALIVE

        CHEERFUL              ENGAGED                ACTIVE

ENJOYABLE        PERSEVERING            ENERGETIC

        CURIOUS              LIVELY              INDUSTRIOUS

SPIRITED              DILIGENT              HAPPY

        STRONG                FULL                VIGOROUS

Add any additional words you think of here:

_____

_____

_____

_____

_____

## WALK

**Right-Now Women remove busy from our lives.** Congratulations on completing Day 6. It's time to walk it out.

Write down what you learned today, what you intend to apply to your life, and what your first step will be to remove busy from your vocabulary and your life. It may be similar to yesterday's Walk.

_____

_____

_____

_____

_____

Well done, Right-Now Woman!

Pray:

*Thank You, God, for enlightening me to the truth that being too busy has no place in my life. It's not Your best for me. Please show me daily how I can live in Your peace and within Your pace. I desire more of You in my life and less of the busyness of this world. May I glorify You as I apply to my life what You're teaching me. Amen.*

Use the space on the next page to journal any additional prayers, thoughts, or insights.

# DAY 7

*Right-Now Women address our distractions
to effectively overcome them.*

## READY

Take a slow, deep breath. Prepare your heart. Ask the Holy Spirit to enlighten your mind, remove distractions, and open your heart to what God has for you today.

Pray:

*Lord, thank You for this time with You. I come with my hands and heart open to what You have for me. Please remove any distractions during this time so I can wholeheartedly focus on You. Holy Spirit, give me eyes to see and a mind to understand and apply what You teach me. Draw me closer to You in these moments. Amen.*

Today and tomorrow, read Chapter 4 of *Right Now Matters*.

## INQUIRE

Before we can focus on overcoming distractions, we must understand what is distracting us in the first place. Back on Day 1, you listed distractions that prevented you from living in the moment and caused you to live distracted. Return to that list for a moment. (You may want to bookmark it for today's study.) Add any distractions you've noticed since making that list.

After reading Chapter 4 of *Right Now Matters* and the explanations and examples of external and internal distractions, mark an "E" next to the external distractions on your list and an "I" next to the internal distractions.

Count your results. Which distractions are greater on your list—external or internal? Write the total number of each here.

External: _____     Internal: _____

Which distraction stands out to you the most? Why do you think it does?

_____

_____

_____

_____

_____

## GIVE

Give yourself permission to pause and examine these distractions. Don't gloss over them, but read them, one by one. Take your time. This is important because becoming aware of them will help you understand exactly what is stealing your attention. This will aid you in overcoming these distractions.

## HEART

Possibly for the first time ever you're becoming aware of the numerous distractions that pull you away from your real life—the abundant life Jesus came to give you. We're not typically trained to notice the distractions in our lives. Instead, we are taught to do more, to be more, to achieve more. When has this ever worked to our advantage? Is this even biblical?

When have we ever been encouraged to live in the moment or been given tangible steps to do so? When have we ever been instructed on how to battle these distractions we experience daily? No one is talking about this—at least not in my life. I was never taught how to recognize distractions, let alone how to overcome them. Not one person ever mentioned to me, even in passing, that distractions were potentially overrunning and overruling my life. But I was instructed to "just do more," to multitask everything, and to sacrifice my self-care to fit more in my day. You, too? We just keep doing what we're doing, thinking this is the way it's always going to be, or maybe—just maybe—someday when we're retired, life won't be this hectic. Why wait until retirement to live an abundant life?

What if we took a different approach? We now know that we're distracted. We've listed what's distracting us and we see it on paper. As we become aware of the distractions that plague us, what if we address them, instead, so we can better defeat them? This is the heart of today's study.

## TRUTH

At the beginning of Chapter 4 of *Right Now Matters,* I share some examples of people in the Bible who were distracted. I encourage you to read through each of these accounts. If time doesn't allow you to do it today, please make time in the days to come to read them. They will encourage you and open your eyes to the reality of how prevalent distractions are—in every age and culture.

Today, however, let's look closer at the story of how Peter was distracted by the wind and the waves in Matthew 14:25-33. Open your Bible and take your time as you read this passage.

Verse 29 shares how Peter climbed out of the boat and walked on the water toward Jesus. In verse 30, what caused him to sink?

_____

_____

_____

_____

What did Jesus do and say to Peter?

_____

_____

_____

_____

Peter could walk on water as long as he kept his focus on Jesus. However, once he took his eyes off Jesus and put it on the distraction—the waves—he sank. Look at your list of distractions again. Which one is most causing you to take your eyes off Jesus and the abundant life He came to give you?

_____

_____

_____

_____

## NEW

Distractions entice us to take our eyes off Jesus to focus on the distraction itself. What new thought or realization is God giving you through your list of distractions, the Bible passages, or both? Write it down here.

_____

_____

_____

_____

_____

## OPEN

Look at your list of distractions once again. Create a pie chart with the circle below for the total amount of time you spend living distracted. Label each section with the distractions that plague you the most. For example, if you feel your phone distracts you the most, estimate how much time it does (25% of your total distractions? 50%?). This will help put your distraction list in perspective. Remember, your total distracted time should equal 100%, even though, thankfully, you aren't distracted 100% of the time.

## WALK

**Right-Now Women address our distractions to effectively overcome them.** This is where the process of living an undistracted life begins—with awareness. Well done on completing Day 7. Now it's time to walk it out.

Write down what you learned from your study today, what you intend to apply to your life, and which distraction tends to plague you the most.

_____

_____

_____

_____

_____

Well done, Right-Now Woman!

Pray:

*Thank You, God, for Your guiding presence today and for enlightening me to the reality of the distractions that pull me away from You and what You have for me. Please continue to make me aware of these distractions, especially the ones that I may be missing. Help me to not get discouraged by them but to trust You as You lead me beyond them. Amen.*

Use the space on the next page to journal any additional prayers, thoughts, or insights.

# DAY 8

*Right-Now Women recognize living intentionally matters because right now matters.*

---

**READY**

Take a slow, deep breath. Prepare your heart. Ask the Holy Spirit to enlighten your mind, remove distractions, and open your heart to what God has for you today.

Pray:

*Lord, You are so good to me. Thank You for teaching me and guiding me in Your ways. You don't leave me as I am, but You continue to mold me into the person You desire me to be. Thank You. Please lead me and guide me into truth today, and Holy Spirit, help me to understand and apply what I'm learning. Please keep distractions away from this time with You. Amen.*

Continue reading Chapter 4 of *Right Now Matters*.

**INQUIRE**

Yesterday we examined our distractions from the list we made on Day 1. We noticed whether they were internal or external distractions and marked them as such. Look at your list again. Are there any distractions you missed and need to add to your list after looking at those in Chapter 4 of *Right Now Matters?* If so, write them down here, then add them to your list.

_____

_____

_____

_____

_____

## GIVE

Give yourself permission to explore ways to overcome these distractions. You don't have to put the ideas into practice today, but be open to them.

## HEART

Think about what you already do to help yourself overcome distractions. In Chapter 4 of *Right Now Matters,* I list the answers from my poll takers and what they do to overcome the distractions in their lives. Read over that list. Do any remind you of something you do? Does one or two stand out to you that you could try?

For several years when I was in my early twenties, I participated in a bowling league on Wednesday nights. I learned right away that my ball preferred gutters. Either that, or my right arm would naturally just roll them in their direction. *Can we just put up the bumpers when it's my turn to bowl?* I wish that would have been an option.

The things we do to overcome distractions, or do in advance to keep the distractions away, are like these bumpers. They keep us from falling into the gutter. They keep us on the path to where we are going. Someday we'll learn how to make it down the lane without them, but for now—we need them. That's what they are there for, so let's utilize them. This is the heart of today's study.

## TRUTH

We can either live randomly or intentionally, accidentally or deliberately. Distractions will appear with either choice, but when we're intentional and deliberate, we will be less likely to be dragged away by those distractions.

When we incorporate ways to overcome distractions, like working from a list or setting a schedule, we are living intentionally and deliberately.

Today we highlight two Scriptures in the New Testament of the Bible that speak to living in this manner. Open your Bible, and find these two passages: Ephesians 5:15-17 and 1 John 5:21. Let's look at them together.

"So be careful how you live. Don't live like fools, but like those who are wise. Make the most of every opportunity in these evil days. Don't act thoughtlessly, but understand what the Lord wants you to do" (Ephesians 5:15-17 NLT).

- When we are careful how we live, we are living intentionally.

- When we live like those who are wise, we are living deliberately.

- When we stop acting thoughtlessly, we are choosing to live purposefully.

How are you being careful in how you live regarding distractions? Is there anything you could do that could be more effective?

_____

_____

_____

_____

_____

"Dear children, keep away from anything that might take God's place in your hearts" (1 John 5:21 NLT).

- When we steer clear from the things that replace God in our lives, we are living on purpose and consciously choosing wisdom.

- Our choices directly impact our lives.

What will you choose to avoid so it doesn't take the place of God in your life?

_____

_____

_____

_____

_____

What other Scriptures come to mind that speak of living intentionally and deliberately?

_____

_____

_____

_____

_____

How does this encourage you today?

_____

_____

_____

_____

_____

## NEW

We don't have to allow distractions to have their way with us. We can do something about them and prepare for them in advance. What new thought or idea is God showing you, either regarding living intentionally or recalling ideas to overcome distractions? Write it down here.

_____

_____

_____

_____

_____

## OPEN

Use this space to doodle or draw pictures of ways you can live intentionally and deliberately to overcome distractions, either from the list in Chapter 4 of *Right Now Matters* or from your own list. It doesn't matter if you're not an artist. (I can't draw for the life of me, but I can draw stick figures—so there's that.) This doesn't have to be perfect. Just open yourself up and get creative. Have fun with this exercise.

## WALK

**Right-Now Women recognize living intentionally matters because right now matters.** Well done on completing Day 8. Now it's time to walk it out.

Write down what you learned from your study today, what you intend to apply to your life, and one idea you're excited to implement regarding overcoming distractions.

_____

_____

_____

_____

_____

Well done, Right-Now Woman!

Pray:

*Thank You, God, for helping me understand that I can do something about these distractions. Please continue to help me in living intentionally and deliberately with You. Guide me and lead me. I'm grateful for Your presence. Amen.*

Use the space on the next page to journal any additional prayers, thoughts, or insights.

_____

_____

_____

_____

_____

_____

_____

_____

_____

_____

_____

_____

_____

_____

_____

_____

_____

_____

# DAY 9

*Right-Now Women understand living in the present—
not the past or the future—is God's best for us.*

## READY

Take a slow, deep breath. Prepare your heart. Ask the Holy Spirit to enlighten your mind, remove distractions, and open your heart to what God has for you today.

Pray:

*Lord, thank You that you are a personal God. You are teaching me and guiding me into this new way of living, and I praise You for it. Thank You for helping me to become aware of the distractions that plague me the most and for teaching me—one step at a time—what to do about them. Please remove any distractions during this time with You. Holy Spirit, open my mind to what You have for me today. Draw me close to You. Amen.*

Today and tomorrow, read Chapter 5 of *Right Now Matters*.

## INQUIRE

After reading Chapter 5 of *Right Now Matters,* which distraction of either The Past or The Future resonates most with you? (We'll look at the last three of The Big Five tomorrow.) Did either one bring about any new emotions, feelings, or memories? Write down your thoughts to acknowledge them.

_____

_____

_____

_____

_____

## GIVE

Give yourself permission to be open to what God might reveal to you as you ponder these two distractions—The Past and The Future—of The Big Five. Is either one of these keeping you stuck or robbing you of your peace and joy? Allow God to use this time to bring awareness and even healing and wholeness into your life.

## HEART

The Past and The Future are two spaces of time we're tempted to dwell on—so much so, they can distract us from the gifts in the present. If our thoughts are stuck on the past, the what ifs, the regrets, and even the good old days, we can't fully enjoy right now. If we're fretting about the future, or our focus is on the hope of what's to come, we are unable to fully appreciate the present. Right now matters because it's the only moment we have.

I share in Chapter 5 of _Right Now Matters_ some instances of how I lived in both the past and the future, and neither served me well. _When have these ever served any of us well?_ Living in the moment and staying present is God's best for us. It always has been and always will be.

## TRUTH

God indicates in His Word how important it is to stay present. Think about all the ways we read in Scripture of how Jesus modeled that for us. Here are a handful:

- He healed numerous people in crowds (Matthew 15:29-31).

- He let the little children come to Him while He was in the middle of speaking to a crowd (Matthew 19:13-15).

- He filled nets with fish after teaching a crowd (Luke 5:1-11).

- He calmed the storm at sea after the disciples woke Him (Luke 8:22-25).

- He turned water into wine at a wedding in Cana (John 2:1-11).

No matter where He was going or what He was doing, Jesus always stayed present—present to notice the needs of others, to share the truth of salvation, and to always be doing the work of His Father.

Open your Bible and read through these accounts above. Which one impacts you the most today and why?

_____

_____

_____

_____

_____

How do these motivate you to not live in the past or the future—but to remain in the present?

_____

_____

_____

_____

_____

## NEW

Right Now Matters, and what we do with it matters. Overcoming the pull to linger in the past or long for the future will help us live how God desires us to right now. What new thought is God giving you about these two distractions, The Past and The Future? Write it out here.

_____

_____

_____

_____

_____

## OPEN

How have you been living in the past or in the future? Take a moment to ask God to reveal to you any ways you have been doing that lately. Again, once we become aware, we can begin the process of addressing the distraction. Write down the ways He reveals to you in the spaces below.

Ways I've been living in the past:

_____

_____

_____

_____

Ways I've been living in the future:

_____

_____

_____

_____

_____

## WALK

**Right-Now Women understand living in the present—and not the past or the future—is God's best for us.** Great job completing Day 9. It's time to walk it out.

Write down what you learned today, what you intend to apply to your life, and which distraction has affected you the most—The Past or The Future.

_____

_____

_____

_____

_____

Well done, Right-Now Woman!

Pray:

*God, I am grateful for this time with You. Thank You for helping me see that Your best for me is to stay present and not to dwell on the past or focus on the future. These two distractions are ones that I don't want to entertain any longer. Please help me daily to overcome them and stay present with You. Amen.*

Use the space on the next page to journal any additional prayers, thoughts, or insights.

# DAY 10

*Right-Now Women realize we can break*
*free from consuming distractions.*

## READY

Take a slow, deep breath. Prepare your heart. Ask the Holy Spirit to enlighten your mind, remove distractions, and open your heart to what God has for you today.

Pray:

*Thank You, Lord, for this day and for this time with You. I praise You for how You are teaching, guiding, and leading me on this path of living undistracted. I'm grateful for Your many blessings and for Your loving presence in my life. Please guide me in today's study, and keep the distractions at bay. Holy Spirit, reveal to me Your truth, and help me to understand what You have for me. Amen.*

Continue reading Chapter 5 of *Right Now Matters*.

## INQUIRE

Yesterday we pondered the first two distractions of The Big Five—The Past and The Future—in Chapter 5 of *Right Now Matters*. Peering into the remaining three distractions today, do any of these grab your attention? Think for a moment. Do you struggle with Technology, Our Thoughts/Ourselves, or Multitasking? If so, which one hinders you the most? Write down your thoughts to acknowledge them.

_____

_____

_____

_____

_____

## GIVE

Give yourself permission to face these three distractions—Technology, Our Thoughts/Ourselves, and Multitasking—and to be okay with any uncomfortable feelings as you do so. It's okay to feel this way. Instead of ignoring these feelings, allow them to surface and give God the opportunity to bring about any healing and wholeness through them.

## HEART

The last three distractions in this chapter of _Right Now Matters_ are big ones for many of us, including me. Do they appear on your list of distractions, too? It's likely we each struggle with them simply because they can be a big part of our everyday lives. Regarding Technology, so much of what we do is centered around technology and our devices. With Our Thoughts/Ourselves, we may be our own biggest distractions! The Harvard study I referenced in Chapter 4 of Right Now Matters states that our thoughts are elsewhere 47% of the time.[1] As we go about our days, Multitasking could be the biggest culprit of all because many of us don't recognize its detrimental effects on our brains. It's no wonder these are three of the biggest distractions!

I don't elaborate personally on Technology in Chapter 5 of _Right Now Matters_ because I don't know where to begin. Every day I work with technology, either through ministry, my writing, or my part-time job. I'm currently the Director of Communication for a church here in Iowa, and most of what I do in that role is centered on technology. I can't escape it! It's not like I can step away from social media for a long measure of time, because that's part of my job. It's difficult to take a break from my laptop for more than a couple of days because much of what I do is accomplished on it.

I've chosen to get creative with ways to halt the distraction of Technology from consuming my life, such as only allowing certain times of day for scrolling, or giving myself boundaries when I'm posting. It took me some time, but I've figured out what works for me. You may need to find creative ways to overcome The Big Five distractions, too. Nonetheless, these are big distractions we are to guard against, no matter how we do it.

## TRUTH

The apostle Paul addressed the church at Corinth regarding various issues, including sexual immorality of that day. We read a verse of his letter in Chapter 5 of *Right Now Matters.* This verse may help us put into perspective anything that may have the power to influence us or control us, even distractions. Open your Bible, and read 1 Corinthians 6:12. Write it out here in the translation you're using.

_____

_____

_____

_____

_____

The Living Bible translation states it this way: "I can do anything I want to if Christ has not said no, but some of these things aren't good for me. Even if I am allowed to do them, I'll refuse to if I think they might get such a grip on me that I can't easily stop when I want to."

These three distractions can easily get a grip on us. Do any have a grip on you? Circle your answers on the next page.

## Technology:

Do you feel you can't live without it? yes | no

Do you panic when you can't find your device or phone? yes | no

Do you spend more time immersed in Technology than anything else in your day? yes | no

## Our Thoughts/Ourselves:

Do you or your thoughts confound, mislead, or trouble you? yes | no

Do your thoughts throughout the day generally distract you? yes | no

Are you constantly thinking, planning, and pondering? yes | no

## Multitasking:

Do you try to multitask often and, as a result, inhibit your effectiveness and creativity? yes | no

Is it difficult for you to not multitask in a typical day? yes | no

Do you often find yourself mentally exhausted at the end of your day? yes | no

If you answered yes to any of the above, I encourage you to take these to God and ask Him to help you begin the process of overcoming these distractions. God does not want you to live under the burden or in bondage of any distraction. He wants to help you break the chains of these things that attempt to keep you ineffective and limited.

## NEW

Right Now Matters, and what we do with it matters. Overcoming these three of The Big Five distractions will help us live the lives God desires us to live. What new thoughts is God showing you about these distractions? What has He revealed to you about them in your life? Write it out here.

_____

_____

_____

_____

_____

## OPEN

What do you think your life would look like if it was absent of the distractions of Technology, Our Thoughts/Ourselves, or Multitasking? Imagine this for a moment and describe it in the blanks below.

My life without these three distractions would look less _____ (anything negative) and more _____ (anything positive).

I would likely feel _____ and _____ (any emotions, attitudes, dispositions, feelings) without these distractions.

In their absence I would no longer be afraid to _____ (dream a little here).

Without them, one thing I would like to try would be _____ (something new or to try again).

I believe my walk with God would _____ (how your relationship with God might improve without them).

I would be more present with _____ (name of someone) in the absence of these three distractions.

## WALK

**Right-Now Women realize we can break free from consuming distractions.** Great job completing Day 10. It's time to walk it out.

Write down what you learned today, what you intend to apply to your life, and which of these three distractions you will focus on eliminating first from your life.

_____

_____

_____

_____

_____

Well done, Right-Now Woman!

Pray:

_God, thank You for meeting me where I am today and for helping me see how living distracted is not Your best for me. I give to You these three distractions, and I ask for Your guidance regarding them. Help me to live free with you, in Your will and Your ways. I trust You. Amen._

Use the space on the next page to journal any additional prayers, thoughts, or insights.

# DAY 11

*Right-Now Women understand God
knows what's best for our lives.*

## READY

Take a slow, deep breath. Prepare your heart. Ask the Holy Spirit to enlighten your mind, remove distractions, and open your heart to what God has for you today.

Pray:

*Lord, You are so good to me. Thank You for always being available and open every time I come to You. Today I am here with a willingness to learn all You want to teach me and how You want to grow me. Please remove all distractions so I can completely focus on You during this next while. Holy Spirit, open my mind to Your truth. Amen.*

Today and tomorrow, read Chapter 6 of *Right Now Matters*.

## INQUIRE

Are you tempted to do things on your own—independently—or would you rather rely on and involve the help of others? Answering this question will aid you in determining your natural tendencies. In Chapter 6 of *Right Now Matters*, I share my natural tendency of independence—both the good and the not-so-good of it. This will be helpful to know for today's study.

## GIVE

Give yourself permission to let go of control, no matter how comfortable or uncomfortable that may feel. This is important because we can trust the

One who is in control of all things, even in helping us live undistracted.

## HEART

We cannot live undistracted on our own. Maybe, like me, you've tried it. No matter how hard we try to fight these distractions by ourselves, we can't effectively succeed at it. Even though we are strong, capable, and talented women, we aren't strong enough, wise enough, or able enough to stand against them alone. God sees what we cannot and knows what we do not. We need God. Period.

It's not always easy to relinquish control, especially if we are the independent type. I remember years ago how an older and wiser friend of mine said, "I'm one who likes to have my ducks in a row, but sometimes I can't even remember where I put them!" I can relate. I habitually like to be in control of my life—until I can't remember where I put my glasses and realize they've been on top of my head the entire time. Or until I get in my car and attempt to start it without the key. It's then that I understand I should not oversee anything, let alone my own life!

Our Creator is infinitely more qualified to oversee and handle our lives than we are.

## TRUTH

I share two Scriptures in Chapter 6 of *Right Now Matters.* The first one is Psalm 25:4-5. As I mention in this chapter, this has become a prayer I say nearly every day. I invite you to open your Bible, locate this Scripture, read it, and write it down here.

_____

_____

_____

_____

The second verse is Psalm 32:8. Turn to that passage, read it, and write it down here.

_____

_____

_____

_____

_____

The New Living Translation states this verse in this way: "The Lord says, 'I will guide you along the best pathway for your life. I will advise you and watch over you.'" Let's break this down and look at it deeper.

What does the Lord say? He says He will guide you and me along the best pathway for our lives. This tells us that He knows the best path for your life and mine. He sees everything. We do not. He knows everything. We do not. He has the entire world in His hands. We do not. He knows what's best for us. We do not.

The second part of that verse tells us that God will advise us—will inform us, warn us, instruct us—and will watch over us. That means He is always with us. He won't leave us to fend for ourselves but instead, He will guide us every step of the way—even in the battle against distractions. He will always guide us to His best for our lives. We can count on that to be true. Isn't that the best news today?

I invite you to place these verses where you can see them each morning to remind you of God's provision and presence in your life.

## NEW

God is our Guide, our source, our strength. And He is the One who keeps us undistracted. What new thought or realization is He revealing to you as you allow Him to be in control of your life and your circumstances? Write it down here.

_____

_____

_____

_____

_____

How did either of the two Scriptures encourage you today?

_____

_____

_____

_____

_____

## OPEN

On the following pages are spheres of life we may try to control. Next to each one is a Bible verse to help us release that control into God's capable hands. Open your Bible and take your time reading through each one. Write them out if that helps you. Keep this list handy to become familiar with these Scriptures. Put an asterisk by the ones you will refer to when you need encouragement in releasing control.

Anxiety: 1 Peter 5:7

_____

_____

_____

_____

Courage: Joshua 1:9

_____

_____

_____

_____

Fear: Isaiah 41:10

_____

_____

_____

_____

Future: Jeremiah 29:11

_____

_____

_____

_____

Peace: John 14:27

_____

_____

_____

_____

Planning: Proverbs 16:9

_____

_____

_____

_____

Purpose: Proverbs 16:4

_____

_____

_____

_____

Safety: Psalm 34:7

_____

_____

_____

_____

Temptation: 1 Corinthians 10:13

_____

_____

_____

_____

Thoughts/Ways: Isaiah 55:8-9

_____

_____

_____

_____

Trouble/Hardship: Psalm 46:1

_____

_____

_____

_____

Vengeance: Romans 12:19

_____

_____

_____

_____

World/Universe: Hebrews 1:3

_____

_____

_____

_____

Worry: Matthew 6:34

_____

_____

_____

_____

## WALK

**Right-Now Women understand that God knows what's best for our lives.** Allowing Him to be in control helps us to live undistracted lives. Congratulations on completing Day 11. Now it's time to walk it out.

Write down what you learned from your study today, what you intend to apply to your life, and how you plan to release control of your life and give it to God.

_____

_____

_____

_____

_____

Well done, Right-Now Woman!

Pray:

*Thank You, God, for showing me how You know the best path for my life and that You will guide me and lead me on that path. I don't want to attempt to live one more day—or hour or minute—without You and Your loving presence. Life with You is an adventure, and I look forward to journeying with You through it. Thank You for loving me like You do. I am grateful. Amen.*

Use the space on the next page to journal any additional prayers, thoughts, or insights.

# DAY 12

*Right-Now Women partner with God daily.*

---

## READY

Take a slow, deep breath. Prepare your heart. Ask the Holy Spirit to enlighten your mind, remove distractions, and open your heart to what God has for you today.

Pray:

*Lord, thank You for not leaving me as I once was or as I am today—but for continuing to mold me into the person You desire for me to be. Thank You for Your grace and love. Holy Spirit, guide me to Your truth, and help me to embrace all You have for me today. Remove any distractions that might try to hinder this time with You. Amen.*

Continue reading Chapter 6 of *Right Now Matters*.

## INQUIRE

If you could describe your relationship with God in one word, what would it be? Be open and honest with yourself in this, and whatever word comes to mind first, allow it to have merit. Write that word here.

_____

_____

_____

_____

## GIVE

Give yourself permission to embrace your relationship with God. The world tells us we don't need God, and our spiritual enemy wants us to make sure we believe that. Some say we should hide our relationship with God to be accepting and inclusive. What do you say? What does your relationship with God mean to you? Take some time to think about this.

## HEART

As we are learning, God is the only One who can help us live undistracted. We need Him in every part of our lives, not just in this area.

In Chapter 6 of *Right Now Matters,* I share how my relationship with God began. It's something I feel is important to share. Not only this—but to also share I haven't walked with God perfectly since. It's been a journey for which I'm grateful.

I can't begin to guess what your relationship with God is like—or whether you have one. But I invite you to either commit to growing that relationship with Him or beginning one. It's not as scary, or weird, or difficult as sometimes we believe. It just takes our willing heart and God's grace. They go well together. I invite you to pray the prayer I wrote on page 91 of *Right Now Matters*—or something similar. I need God every single day of my life, and friend, if I can be so bold to proclaim so—you need Him, too. We all do.

## TRUTH

Our relationship with God matters—not just for life right now, but for eternity. John 3:16-18 reads, "For God so loved the world that he gave his one and only Son, that whoever believes in him shall not perish but have eternal life. For God did not send his Son into the world to condemn the world, but to save the world through him. Whoever believes in him is not condemned, but whoever does not believe stands condemned already because they have not believed in the name of God's one and only Son." This Scripture points us to the truth of how to have a relationship with Jesus and why that's so important.

Open your Bible to John 15:1-8. Read this passage and write down key words or phrases that stand out to you.

_____

_____

_____

_____

_____

Jesus states here that He is the true vine, and God is the gardener. We are branches of the vine, and God does the work of pruning us, so we can flourish and be more fruitful. Apart from the vine, we will wither and die. We simply can't do anything unattached from the vine. When we stay attached to the vine, however, we will receive all we need to bear fruit and glorify God.

I understand life apart from the vine. From personal experience, I know what it's like to feel the withering and drying up inside—and the inability to do anything worthwhile as a result of being detached from Jesus. Remaining in Jesus is the key! Jesus is the way to a relationship with God and the means by Whom we mature in Him.

I also know how it feels to be pruned. Maybe you do as well. The pruning seasons may be painful, but we can look back and see the fruit that came from them. We are changed through these seasons. When God prunes us, He does it for our growth, for the good of others, and for His glory. He also holds us close during the pruning seasons.

I'm reminded of my marigolds that are currently in bloom. Every day I pluck off or "deadhead" the spent flowers—those that are done blooming. If I don't, new growth and reflowering of the plant will come to a halt. Pretty soon all that would remain would be a green bush with no bright flowers. The other day I noticed one of the stems had broken off the plant. It was withering and turning brown because it was no longer receiving life from the stem.

The same goes for us. God prunes us for new growth and reflowering. This is a good thing. But more importantly, if we break off from the plant (the vine, Jesus), we, too, will wither and turn brown from not receiving the life found in Him. Remaining in Jesus is the only way to live an abundant, flourishing life.

## NEW

With us, God may have His hands full, but I believe He'd rather have them full than empty. What new thought or realization is God revealing to you as you contemplate committing to a deeper relationship with Him or beginning a relationship with Him? Write it out here.

_____

_____

_____

_____

## OPEN

Open your heart to God and write a letter to Him about your relationship with Him. Don't worry about punctuation or grammar or even if it makes complete sense. Allow whatever is on your heart and in your mind to come out through your hand and onto the paper. This is just between you and God. Take a deep breath, and write.

Dear God,

_____

_____

_____

_____

_____

_____

_____

_____

_____

_____

_____

_____

_____

_____

Love,

## WALK

**Right-Now Women partner with God daily.** We don't do this perfectly, but we know we cannot experience a fulfilling and abundant life without Him. Congratulations on completing Day 12. Now it's time to walk it out.

Write down what you learned from your study today, what you intend to apply to your life, and what you will do next in your relationship with God.

_____

_____

_____

_____

_____

Well done, Right-Now Woman!

Pray:

*Thank You, God, for helping me see the importance of a relationship with You. I need You in my life. Help me to take Your hand and walk with you daily. Show me how I can live this abundant life Jesus came to give me. Thank You for drawing me to You and Your truth today. I am grateful. Amen.*

Use the space on the next page to journal any additional prayers, thoughts, or insights.

# DAY 13

*Right-Now Women begin our days with God.*

## READY

Take a slow, deep breath. Prepare your heart. Ask the Holy Spirit to enlighten your mind, remove distractions, and open your heart to what God has for you today.

Pray:

*Lord, thank You for this day and this moment. You have the entire world in Your hands, yet it boggles my mind how You desire to spend time with me. I am ready for what You have for me today, and I look forward to learning from You. Please take away any distractions that try to interrupt this time. Holy Spirit, open my mind and my heart to receive and understand Your truth. Amen.*

Today and tomorrow, read Chapter 7 of *Right Now Matters*.

## INQUIRE

How do you begin your day? Do you have a typical routine? How would you describe it? Write down your answers here.

_____

_____

_____

_____

_____

## GIVE

Give yourself permission to open your schedule to God and to be flexible with what He might show you regarding spending time with Him.

## HEART

In Chapter 6 of *Right Now Matters,* we learn how the path to living undistracted begins with God. The next natural step is beginning each day with God. This may look differently for each one of us, and depending on our schedules and life routines, some days we must be flexible. Do you typically begin your day with God? Or do you spend time with Him at some point through your day?

In past years, I began my day with exercise, then I followed it with time with God. In other years when our children were young, my time with God resembled a different routine. I couldn't always begin my day in silence with God when our children were early risers, but I found other times throughout the day. I even remember reading my Bible in the pick-up line at school or praying during my lunch break.

If beginning your day with God isn't possible for you, please don't let that stop you from spending time with Him. God will guide You as you seek His direction to determine the best time for you to spend with Him.

## TRUTH

Have you ever done a word search in the Bible? Open your Bible to its concordance (if it has one) and look for Bible verses regarding "morning." Or do a search on your device or computer for "Bible verses about morning." (Be careful not to get distracted by anything else on your device or computer, however. I know how easily that can happen!) Locate two or three verses that the Holy Spirit highlights for you. Write them down here.

_____

_____

_____

_____

_____

_____

Which Bible verse helps you see the value of beginning your day with God?

_____

_____

_____

_____

Psalm 143:8 does that for me. It reads, "Let the morning bring me word of your unfailing love, for I have put my trust in you. Show me the way I should go, for to you I entrust my life." This verse reminds me of the importance of going to God right away in the morning, because remembering His unfailing love keeps my heart and mind secure in His peace. I also know what happens when I try to figure out the way I should go on my own each day instead of allowing God to show me. It never fails, on the mornings when my time with God is either rushed or nonexistent, I feel like a fish out of water. I'm a bit lost. I miss God's peace, presence, and provision if I omit that time with Him in the morning.

We rise early for things that are important to us. Whether it's an early-morning cry from the crib in the baby's room, an early alarm to catch a plane, or a before-sunrise view of a once-in-a-lifetime lunar eclipse, we wake for what matters.

Jesus was the Master at this. He knew what mattered and rose early for it.

Mark 1:35 tells us, "Very early in the morning, while it was still dark, Jesus got up, left the house and went off to a solitary place, where he prayed."

We can learn from Jesus here. What if we rose while it was still dark to spend time with our Creator, our Heavenly Father? Could we? Would we? This time of quiet alone with God benefits us before the world's noise of the day tries to drown out His voice.

Not only did Jesus rise early then, but have you ever noticed that He also rose early at the end of the book of Mark? "Very early on the first day of the week, just after sunrise, they were on their way to the tomb, and they asked each other, 'Who will roll the stone away from the entrance of the tomb?' But when they looked up, they saw that the stone, which was very large, had been rolled away" (Mark 16:2-4). Jesus rose early from the tomb in the same manner. He knew what mattered and rose early for it. If He did, maybe it's wise for us to consider the same.

## NEW

Each day we need God's equipping and guidance if we are going to overcome distractions that try to steer us off course. What new thought or direction is God showing you regarding your time with Him? Write it out here.

_____

_____

_____

_____

_____

## OPEN

Look at your typical week. Plug your schedule into the blocks on this calendar with as many commitments, activities, and appointments as you possibly can—even your wake and sleep times. Even your breakfast, lunch, and dinner times, and your time with God (if you have that at this point). If your weeks are anything like mine, they vary, but try to fill it out for a typical week in your life.

|      | Mon | Tues | Wed | Thurs | Fri | Sat | Sun |
|------|-----|------|-----|-------|-----|-----|-----|
| 12a  |     |      |     |       |     |     |     |
| 1    |     |      |     |       |     |     |     |
| 2    |     |      |     |       |     |     |     |
| 3    |     |      |     |       |     |     |     |
| 4    |     |      |     |       |     |     |     |
| 5    |     |      |     |       |     |     |     |
| 6    |     |      |     |       |     |     |     |
| 7    |     |      |     |       |     |     |     |
| 8    |     |      |     |       |     |     |     |
| 9    |     |      |     |       |     |     |     |
| 10   |     |      |     |       |     |     |     |
| 11   |     |      |     |       |     |     |     |
| 12p  |     |      |     |       |     |     |     |
| 1    |     |      |     |       |     |     |     |
| 2    |     |      |     |       |     |     |     |
| 3    |     |      |     |       |     |     |     |
| 4    |     |      |     |       |     |     |     |
| 5    |     |      |     |       |     |     |     |
| 6    |     |      |     |       |     |     |     |
| 7    |     |      |     |       |     |     |     |
| 8    |     |      |     |       |     |     |     |
| 9    |     |      |     |       |     |     |     |
| 10   |     |      |     |       |     |     |     |
| 11   |     |      |     |       |     |     |     |

Looking at your typical schedule, where do you or can you add dedicated time with God to your schedule? Can you make time with Him a priority as you begin your day? What does that look like for you? Write any thoughts or realizations here.

_____

_____

_____

_____

_____

## WALK

**Right-Now Women begin our days with God.** We don't do it perfectly, and some days it might not look like we want it to, but we know the value of going to our Heavenly Father first thing. Good job on completing Day 13. Now it's time to walk it out.

Write down what you learned today, what you intend to apply to your life, and how you plan to begin your days with God. (If you aren't able to begin your day with God, when will you plan to spend time with Him?)

_____

_____

_____

_____

Well done, Right-Now Woman!

Pray:

*Thank You, God, for guiding me to Your truth today and for teaching me the value and importance of beginning my days with You. Will You please continue to help me walk this out and show me how to do this, Lord? I look forward to this time with You every day. Thank You. Amen.*

Use the space on the next page to journal any additional prayers, thoughts, or insights.

# DAY 14

*Right-Now Women connect with God in His Word.*

---

## READY

Take a slow, deep breath. Prepare your heart. Ask the Holy Spirit to enlighten your mind, remove distractions, and open your heart to what God has for you today.

Pray:

*Lord, I give You all praise and thanks today for walking with me on this journey of living undistracted. In Your faithfulness, You continue to guide me and teach me how to live differently than I've been living. Please help me to learn what You intend for me to learn today. Holy Spirit, please lead me to understand and apply truth. Keep my mind focused on You during this time. Amen.*

Continue reading Chapter 7 of *Right Now Matters*.

## INQUIRE

When you read a passage of Scripture, what do you typically do with it? Do you try to apply it to your life? Or when you read Scripture and it doesn't make sense or you don't fully understand its meaning, what do you do? Write down your thoughts here.

_____

_____

_____

_____

## GIVE

Give yourself permission to be open to learning a new way to study Scripture. In today's study, we explore a tool that will aid us in understanding and applying Scripture to our current circumstances in life.

## HEART

Wherever we are, God meets us. In Chapter 7 of *Right Now Matters,* I share a method of studying the Bible. For years I was involved in a global, in-depth Bible study called Bible Study Fellowship. There I learned the method of asking three questions after reading a passage of Scripture:

1. What are the facts? (What's happening in this passage?)

2. What are the lessons? (What can I learn from this passage?)

3. What are the applications? (How can I apply this passage to my life right now?)

Facts. Lessons. Applications. When I began to ask these three questions as I read my Bible, Scripture came "alive" for me. I was better able to understand what I was reading, and this allowed me to learn how to apply Scripture to my life. Isn't that what we want to do with the Bible? We don't want to just read words that don't make sense to us, we desire to learn from it, to understand God's Word, and to be able to glean how it matters to our lives right now.

## TRUTH

Ready to give this method a try? Let's walk through it together. Open your Bible to the Scripture passage we read in Chapter 7 of *Right Now Matters,* then answers the three questions below it.

"And you, *beloved,* are the light of the world. A city built on a hilltop cannot be hidden. Similarly it would be silly to light a lamp and then hide it under a bowl. When someone lights a lamp, she puts it on a table or a desk or a chair, and the light illumines the entire house. *You are like that illuminating light.* Let your light shine everywhere you go, *that you may illumine creation,* so men and women everywhere may see your good actions, *may see creation at its fullest, may see your devotion to Me,* and may turn and praise your Father in heaven *because of it"* (Matthew 5:14-16 Voice).

**Question 1:** What are the facts? (What's happening in the passage?)

I'll add a fact: a city on a hill can't be hidden.

List additional facts you see.

_____

_____

_____

_____

_____

_____

**Question 2:** What are the lessons? (What can I learn from this passage?)

Here's a lesson I see: I am to let my light shine everywhere I go.

List any other lessons you notice.

_____

_____

_____

_____

_____

**Question 3:** What are the applications? (How can I apply this passage to my life right now?)

An application for me: Jesus calls me not to hide my light but to shine it into the lives of others so I can ultimately glorify God.

List any other applications that pertain to you.

_____

_____

_____

_____

_____

_____

Learning how to study the Bible and apply it to your life doesn't have to be weird or complicated. This method can help. Try it with any verse of Scripture. I encourage you to write down your answers. The more you do it, the easier it will become. It may just transform your Bible reading time like it did mine!

## NEW

God will guide us as we open His Word and begin to immerse ourselves in it. What new thought or revelation is God showing you regarding this simple method of studying Scripture? Write it out here.

_____

_____

_____

_____

_____

## OPEN

Not sure which Bible passages to read next? Maybe you want to try this method out a few more times to get the hang of it. Or maybe you could simply use some encouragement, hope, or joy right now. Below are some Bible verses divided into categories. Choose one from whichever category you need the most. If you want to use this method of asking three questions and writing down your answers, grab a notebook or use the blank page at the end of this day's study. Open your Bible, and be blessed. Keep this list handy for whenever you may need it in the future.

| Courage | Purpose | Stress | Encouragement |
|---|---|---|---|
| Joshua 1:9 | Philippians 3:8-12 | Isaiah 41:10 | Psalm 77:11-12 |
| Psalm 27:1 | 1 Timothy 6:11-12 | Matthew 11:28-30 | Psalm 86:15 |
| Isaiah 40:29-31 | 2 Timothy 4:7-8 | Mark 6:31 | Proverbs 16:3 |
| Isaiah 43:2 | 1 Peter 3:12-14 | Galatians 6:9 | Lamentations 3:21-23 |

| Wisdom | Priorities | Relationships | Dependence on God |
|---|---|---|---|
| Psalm 32:8 | Psalm 31:19 | Ecclesiastes 4:9-12 | Psalm 34:8 |
| Proverbs 2:1-6 | Philippians 2:2-5 | Romans 12:3-5 | Isaiah 26:3-4 |
| Proverbs 3:5-7 | Hebrews 12:1-2 | Colossians 3:13 | Jeremiah 17:7-8 |
| Proverbs 4:11-12 | Hebrews 13:20-21 | Titus 2:7-8 | Romans 4:20-21 |

## WALK

**Right-Now Women connect with God in His Word.** We understand the value of doing so. The more we do it, the closer our relationship to God will be. Good job on completing Day 14. Now it's time to walk it out.

Write down what you learned today, what you intend to apply to your life, and how you plan to connect with God in His Word.

_____

_____

_____

_____

_____

Well done, Right-Now Woman!

Pray:

*Thank You, God, for guiding me to a simple way to connect with You through the Bible—Your written Word. I look forward to using this method and learning it better. Thank You for teaching me Your truth and blessing me with this time with You. Amen.*

Use the space on the next page to journal any additional prayers, thoughts, or insights.

# DAY 15

*Right-Now Women end our days with God.*

---

## READY

Take a slow, deep breath. Prepare your heart. Ask the Holy Spirit to enlighten your mind, remove distractions, and open your heart to what God has for you today.

Pray:

*Lord, I praise You today for every single blessing and for Your presence in my life. I thank You in advance for this time with You. Please calm my heart, open my mind to Your truth, and allow me to learn whatever it is You desire for me today. Holy Spirit, speak to me and help me be sensitive to Your leading. Please keep any distractions away during this time with You. Amen.*

Today and tomorrow, read Chapter 8 of *Right Now Matters.*

## INQUIRE

How do you typically end the day? Do you have an end-of-day routine? Write down any details or thoughts about it here.

_____

_____

_____

_____

_____

## GIVE

Give yourself permission to think about your evenings, nights, and rest, and to be open about any prompting from God about them.

## HEART

God designed our bodies to rest. We need rest for our physical, mental, emotional, and spiritual health. We need it to be strengthened and alert to do what God calls us to do and to live life in His abundance. Do you protect rest as something you value and enjoy? Do you make rest a priority?

For years I sacrificed sleep to accomplish more. I thought that was the solution. Especially through numerous Christmas seasons when I felt as if I didn't have enough hours in the day to accomplish all I needed to do. Because I didn't take care of myself by protecting my sleep and rest, it wasn't uncommon for me to end up ill on many a Christmas morning. Was sacrificing my sleep and rest worth it? Absolutely not. Our bodies need rest. Period.

It's no secret, when we are tired or weary from lack of rest, we will also be more easily distracted. We aren't mentally equipped to prepare for or fight off daily distractions when we're tired. Not only this, but when we're fatigued, we aren't our best selves. God makes rest a priority. As we noted on Day 2 of our study, He rested on the seventh day of creation. It would be wise for us to make this a priority, too.

## TRUTH

Numerous verses in the Bible refer to sleep and rest. I've listed three here. Open your Bible, read the passages, and write them out to keep for later.

Psalm 3:5

_____

_____

_____

_____

Psalm 127:2

_____

_____

_____

_____

Matthew 11:28-30

_____

_____

_____

_____

These encourage me. Do they do the same for you? We see in Psalm 3:5 how God sustains us through rest. Psalm 127:2 reminds us how sleep is a gift from God to His beloved. Matthew 11:28-30 points us to the truth that rest is available through Jesus as we partner and live our lives with Him. Which one encourages you the most regarding rest? Why?

_____

_____

_____

_____

Could you read one of these tonight before bed to help prepare your heart, soul, and mind for rest? How could you incorporate this into your bed-time routine?

_____

_____

_____

_____

_____

Ending the day with God is just as important as beginning it with Him. Praying, reading Scripture, and drawing near to God helps us keep our focus on what's important and not on the distractions that can bother us at night. Asking God for *His* rest before falling asleep is a fantastic way to release any cares and concerns into the hand of the One who can handle them.

## NEW

Sleep and rest aren't luxuries; they are necessities—so much so, God knows we need them and instructs us about them in His Word. What new thought or revelation is God blessing you with regarding your sleep and rest? Write it out here.

_____

_____

_____

_____

_____

## OPEN

In Chapter 8 of *Right Now Matters,* I share some ways to prepare for a good night's sleep and alleviate distractions. Let's brainstorm and dream a little here. If you could design your perfect evening as you prepare to sleep and as you retire for the day, what would it look like? Would you light a candle and play soft music? Would you drink some soothing tea? How about cuddling under your favorite blanket with your Bible or another good book? List your ideas below. Be sure to include your ideal sleep and wake times.

_____

_____

_____

_____

_____

_____

_____

Now that you've created in your mind and on paper your ideal way to end your day, what's one thing you can do tonight to take a step toward this ideal plan?

_____

_____

_____

_____

## WALK

**Right-Now Women end our days with God.** Good job on completing Day 15. Now it's time to walk it out.

Write down what you learned today, what you intend to apply to your life, and how you plan to end your day with God.

_____

_____

_____

_____

_____

Well done, Right-Now Woman!

Pray:

_Thank You, God, for Your guidance regarding rest and sleep, and for helping me see I need to make these a priority. Would You please continue to help me walk this out and to get the rest I need—Your rest? I look forward to ending my day with You tonight. Amen._

Use the space on the next page to journal any additional prayers, thoughts, or insights.

# DAY 16

*Right-Now Women entrust God with everything.*

## READY

Take a slow, deep breath. Prepare your heart. Ask the Holy Spirit to enlighten your mind, remove distractions, and open your heart to what God has for you today.

Pray:

*Thank You, God, for caring about both the little and big details of my life—and for helping me live a life of Your peace and abundance. I am grateful for Your teaching and equipping. Holy Spirit, lead me today to what You have for me, and transform my thinking through Your truth. Take away any distractions that may try to entice me away from this time with You. I love You, Lord. Amen.*

Continue reading Chapter 8 of *Right Now Matters*.

## INQUIRE

What distractions keep you awake at night, and what do you tend to do about them, if anything? Ponder this for a moment and write your answer here.

_____

_____

_____

_____

_____

## GIVE

Give yourself permission to entrust God with everything including any nighttime distractions so you can overcome them with His help.

## HEART

The distractions we face aren't present just during the daylight hours. Some of the biggest ones knock on the door of our lives at night. I share in Chapter 8 of *Right Now Matters* a few nighttime distractions I've dealt with in past years—clear back to my teenage years—and even more recently.

I can't stress enough how important it is to end our day with God, not only to close out the day in a wonderful way—but to also give every single distraction over to Him. Just because the daytime hours end, it doesn't mean the distractions will leave when the sun goes down. Oftentimes it can be just the opposite. When our bodies are less active at night, it's then that our brains can begin to shift into overdrive—thinking, planning, strategizing, wondering, fretting. You name it—we've done it.

Because we entrust God with everything, we can hand all of that thinking, planning, and fretting over to Him. We can ask Him to take every care and concern and to remove the distractions that try to keep us awake all night long. But will we? Will we truly trust Him and surrender them?

## TRUTH

I found a few Scriptures that might prompt us to trust God with everything including nighttime distractions. They also might help us realize we don't have to contend with them one night longer. Open your Bible to the passages below. Read them slowly, and write them out to keep for later.

Psalm 55:22

_____

_____

_____

_____

Philippians 4:6-7

_____

_____

_____

_____

_____

2 Timothy 1:7

_____

_____

_____

_____

Which one encourages your heart the most right now? Why?

_____

_____

_____

_____

_____

How will you use these verses tonight as you retire for the evening?

_____

_____

_____

_____

## NEW

God wants you to bring every care and concern—even every distraction—to Him. I invite you to take it all to Him at night. What new idea or thought is God revealing to you regarding any nighttime distractions? Write it out here.

_____

_____

_____

_____

_____

## OPEN

Do you ever take a Scripture and pray it? Let's try it now. Examine the three Scriptures in the Truth section of today's study. Pick one, and turn it into a prayer. It doesn't have to be long or elaborate; many Bible verses can be simply read as a prayer, especially the psalms. Write it out as a prayer in the space below, and feel free to do this with the other two Scriptures.

_____

_____

_____

_____

_____

_____

_____

_____

_____

_____

This is a beautiful way to communicate and partner with God.

## WALK

**Right-Now Women entrust God with everything.** Good job on completing Day 16. Now it's time to walk it out.

Write down what you learned today, what you intend to apply to your life, and how you plan to trust God with any nighttime distractions.

_____

_____

_____

_____

Well done, Right-Now Woman!

Pray:

*Lord God, I thank You for how You are willing to take all my cares, burdens, and distractions at any time of day, especially at night. Please prompt me to hand them over to You when I forget, and remind me that I can trust You with everything. You are so good to me, and I am so grateful. Thank You for continuing to teach me and guide me. Amen.*

Use the space on the next page to journal any additional prayers, thoughts, or insights.

# DAY 17

*Right-Now Women apply helpful tools
to aid us in living undistracted.*

## READY

Take a slow, deep breath. Prepare your heart. Ask the Holy Spirit to enlighten your mind, remove distractions, and open your heart to what God has for you today.

Pray:

*Lord, I thank You for this new day. Thank You for inviting me to learn from You and to appreciate Your presence. Holy Spirit, guide my thoughts to focus on what You have for me. Please remove any distractions that may tempt me to turn my attention elsewhere. Lead me in Your truth. Amen.*

Today and tomorrow, read Chapter 9 of *Right Now Matters*.

## INQUIRE

How often do you notice what's going on around you and what's happening in your environment? Do you pay attention to this often, or do you tend to not notice? Reflect on this and write down any thoughts or realizations.

_____

_____

_____

_____

## GIVE

Give yourself permission to lift your eyes more often and to notice your surroundings. This will help in counting blessings and in overcoming distractions.

## HEART

In Chapter 9 of *Right Now Matters,* I share four tools that help me live undistracted. Today we're studying the first two, and tomorrow we'll look at the last two. Keep in mind that you and I are different, and what may work for me, may not work for you. But I believe in these so much, we're taking our time walking through them. God might even inspire you with a fresh idea as we do. This is how these came to be in my life, so listen for God's still, small voice as we walk through them together.

The first tool, Write It Down, is simplistic, isn't it? There's nothing in-depth or fancy about it. Every time I mention it, either while speaking to a group or with an individual, I get the same interesting look as if I'm speaking something so elementary or silly. I can't blame them, because truly, this tool sounds too simple to be effective.

What I normally say to those with inquisitive looks is, "Just try it. It's super simple, but it works." Practice noticing your blessings as well as the distractions. Write them down somewhere throughout your day—on a piece of paper, in a notebook, or somewhere in your phone. Noticing the blessings helps you realize how much goodness you have in your life, and noticing the distractions helps you overcome them. Try it for a day, and see what happens.

The second tool, Use the Four Ps, is another simple one, but it has a few more steps to it. It involves pausing your physical, mental, and emotional pace. That's the Pause part. The Ponder part is what we just talked about— noticing what's happening around you. What do you see, hear, feel, taste, or touch? The third P is Pray. Talk to God about what you noticed, and bring Him into your day and situation. God loves it when you spend time with Him. The fourth part is Praise. Praise God for what you noticed and for what you prayed. Repeat this as often as needed throughout your day to keep yourself focused and undistracted. These are beautiful tools to keep you in the moment.

What stands out to you with either of these two tools? Which one intrigues you the most to the point you want to give it a try?

_____

_____

_____

_____

_____

Is another idea coming to your mind that God might be revealing to you as a tool for your own use? Write it down here.

_____

_____

_____

_____

_____

## TRUTH

God's Word has much to say about pausing, pondering, praying, and praising.

**Pause:** Have you ever noticed a word at the end of some passages in the Old Testament? For years I didn't know what it meant and never bothered to look it up. That word is *Selah,* which means pause. I don't know about you, but I could use more *Selah* in my life. Especially lately.

This Hebrew word is an intentional pause in reading. I understand people disagree whether *Selah* should be read out loud, or if it's simply there to help us pause and reflect on the text. Either way, *Selah* is there for a reason—74 times in the New King James Bible.

How can we add more *Selah* to our lives? One way is to intentionally pause with the Four Ps.

**Ponder:** When I think of ponder, I'm drawn to Luke 2:19 when the shepherds followed the star to Bethlehem and found Mary, Joseph, and Baby Jesus. Open your Bible, and read it with me, starting in verse 17. "When they had seen him, they spread the word concerning what had been told them about this child, and all who heard it were amazed at what the shepherds said to them. But Mary treasured up all these things and pondered them in her heart."

Mary pondered. She considered what she heard, saw, and experienced. We might call it speculating, or evaluating, or mulling it over in our minds. Scripture doesn't clarify what "all these things" were, nor does it say if she ever voiced them. I'm guessing she took her ponderings to her Heavenly Father. It's good for us to do that, too.

**Pray:** The Bible is full of examples of prayer. I appreciate how Colossians Chapter 4 encourages us in this practice. Verse 2 says, "Devote yourselves to prayer, being watchful and thankful." This isn't a once-a-day kind of thing, according to this verse. It's dedicating ourselves and committing our energies to prayer, including being watchful (undistracted) and thankful. One way we can do this throughout our day is to apply this third step in the Four Ps—Pray.

**Praise:** Psalm 150 is all about praising God. Turn to this psalm in your Bible, and take a moment to read it. It encourages us to praise God for—and with—numerous things—in His sanctuary, in His mighty heavens, of His power, and with musical instruments and dancing. It culminates in verse 6: "Let everything that has breath praise the Lord. Praise the Lord." We are a part of that "everything." Following the Four Ps can help us Praise more every day.

When we Pause, Ponder, Pray, and Praise, we not only stay present and live in the moment, but we intentionally grow our relationship with our Lord. How can you incorporate this practice into your life today? Is this something you could try at your breakfast, lunch, and dinner times daily? Get creative, and write down your ideas here.

_____

_____

_____

_____

_____

_____

## NEW

When we stop the rhythm and flow of the day to practice the tools of Write it Down or Pause, Ponder, Pray, and Praise, it's as if we document the day in an entirely new way. What new thought is God giving you about these two tools? How can you incorporate them in your life to help you live undistracted and grow your relationship with God? Write it out here.

_____

_____

_____

_____

_____

## OPEN

Now is a good time to put into practice what we just learned using the Four Ps. Follow the prompts with the spaces below as you Pause, Ponder, Pray, and Praise.

**Pause** in this moment. Write out anything that comes to mind.

_____

_____

_____

_____

_____

**Ponder** all you notice. Write it out below.

_____

_____

_____

_____

**Pray** about what you pondered. Write it out below.

_____

_____

_____

_____

_____

**Praise** God for the focus of your prayer. Write it out below.

_____

_____

_____

_____

_____

## WALK

**Right-Now Women apply helpful tools to aid us in living undistracted.** Great job completing Day 17. It's time to walk it out.

Write down what you learned today, what you intend to apply to your life, and how you plan to apply either of these tools—or any other tools God revealed—to your life.

_____

_____

_____

_____

_____

_____

Well done, Right-Now Woman!

Pray:

*Thank You, God, for meeting me and equipping me with practical tools. You never leave me to fend for myself, but You always provide what I need, when I need it. I am so grateful for You. I praise Your Holy Name today. Amen.*

Use the space on the next page to journal any additional prayers, thoughts, or insights.

# DAY 18

*Right-Now Women use simple tools to help us refocus.*

---

## READY

Take a slow, deep breath. Prepare your heart. Ask the Holy Spirit to enlighten your mind, remove distractions, and open your heart to what God has for you today.

Pray:

*Thank You, Lord, for Your continued faithfulness and goodness towards me. I praise You for how You are leading me each moment of the day. As I draw near to You through Your Word, Holy Spirit, teach me and guide me and my thinking. Please keep distractions away from me during this time with You. Amen.*

Continue reading Chapter 9 of *Right Now Matters*.

## INQUIRE

When you think about the significance of today, what comes to mind? Do you consider today important, or does it just blend in with the other days of the week and month? Write down your thoughts here.

_____

_____

_____

_____

Next, think about the times when life feels overwhelming—or when your brain is filled with items on your to-do list or your numerous responsibilities and commitments. What do you typically do? Write it out here.

_____

_____

_____

_____

_____

## GIVE

Give yourself permission to be open to learning two more tools that can help you live an undistracted life and remain in the moment.

## HEART

Chapter 9 of *Right Now Matters* is titled, "Tools to Refocus." Think about the word *refocus*. It indicates the action of putting something into focus again, something that once was focused but maybe has somehow become blurred. Living in a distraction-filled world can make it difficult for us to consistently keep our focus on what's important. The last two tools in Chapter 9 of *Right Now Matters* may help us.

The third tool, Today's Date, is another simple way to keep ourselves in the moment—or at least in the day. *What day of the week is it, anyway? And what's today's date?* I can't tell you how many times I had to look at my phone to answer these questions before using this tool. This surfaced because of the frustration I experienced regarding that. It's amazing to me how using this tool keeps me focused on today and helps me separate one day from another.

The last tool is one of my favorites: Brain Dump. I use this one all the time. Seriously—almost every day. My brain feels exceedingly full some days, and on other days my schedule causes me to feel overloaded and overwhelmed. There's just something about putting on paper everything running through my mind. This tool frees up my brain, helps me alleviate feelings of overload, and aids me in focusing on what's important.

After learning of these last two tools in Chapter 9 of *Right Now Matters,* what stands out to you regarding them? Which one makes the most sense and appears to be the most helpful to you?

_____

_____

_____

_____

_____

Is God revealing another idea of a tool for you to use? He might have something that's ideal just for you. Ponder this, and write it down here.

_____

_____

_____

_____

_____

## TRUTH

Today matters. What we do with today matters. How we view today matters. This is one reason why it's important to separate it from every other day. We are here, right now, today.

God created this today; that's the main reason why it's important, isn't it? He creates every day. Psalm 118:24 reads, "This is the day the Lord has made. We will rejoice and be glad in it" (NLT).

This verse is one of my friend's favorites. She wakes up every morning and quotes it. Yes, God has made this day, and it's a gift to rejoice and be glad in it. In studying this Scripture further, the psalmist wrote this chapter as a Messianic psalm, referring to the Messiah. In its original language, this verse doesn't acknowledge our twenty-four-hour day, but rather what is referred to as "The Day of the Lord." The Day of the Lord is the day that's already marked in eternity. It's unknown to us, but it's The Day when Jesus returns as the Scriptures say He will, in the clouds for those who believe in Him. No wonder "we will rejoice and be glad in it"!

But this verse can still encourage us regarding the twenty-four-hour period of our days. The original context of this verse is even more hope-filled and powerful. It's much more than today as it's the day we who believe in Jesus look forward to.

Nonetheless, today is important. It's important to live fully in it.

As we peer into the fourth tool in Chapter 9 of *Right Now Matters,* Brain Dump, I can't help but think of Philippians 4:6-7. We looked at these verses in our Day 16 study, but open your Bible and read them again. Write the passage out here.

---

---

---

_____

_____

The peace of God is what I experience each time I use this tool because I don't just dump what's in my brain onto paper. It's much more than that. Like I mention in Chapter 9 of *Right Now Matters,* I use this tool in partnership with God, and I invite Him into my circumstances. I use it as a time of prayer and drawing close to God. He meets me every time. In turn, I receive His peace that goes beyond my understanding. This might be my favorite tool! In a moment you'll get an opportunity to try it out.

## NEW

Aren't each of our moments important? What new thought is God giving you about these two tools? How can you use them in your life to help you live undistracted and grow your relationship with Him? Write it out here.

_____

_____

_____

_____

_____

## OPEN

Let's give one of these tools a try: Brain Dump. Set a timer for five or ten minutes, then write down everything that's running through your mind in the space on the next page. (You can also do this through your device or computer. I just prefer the paper version. For me, there's something about seeing it all in my own handwriting.) Don't worry about punctuation, grammar, or even if it makes sense. Just get it out. Ready? Go!

Next, invite God in. Talk with Him about what you wrote down, and ask Him to align your thoughts with His. Thank Him for releasing you of any burdens and feelings of overwhelm. Don't you feel an immediate difference?

## WALK

**Right-Now Women use simple tools to help us refocus.** Great job completing Day 18. It's time to walk it out.

Write down what you learned today, what you intend to apply to your life, and how you plan to use either of these tools—or any other tools God revealed—in your life.

_____

_____

_____

_____

_____

Well done, Right-Now Woman!

Pray:

_God, thank You for this time with You and for what You taught me today. Help me to continue walking on this path of undistracted living through Your love, grace, and mercy. I love You. Amen._

Use the space on the next page to journal any additional prayers, thoughts, or insights.

_____

_____

_____

_____

_____

_____

_____

_____

_____

_____

_____

_____

_____

_____

_____

_____

_____

_____

_____

_____

# DAY 19

*Right-Now Women understand our focus matters.*

## READY

Take a slow, deep breath. Prepare your heart. Ask the Holy Spirit to enlighten your mind, remove distractions, and open your heart to what God has for you today.

Pray:

*I praise You and thank You, Lord, for this time I get to spend with You, learning from You and being equipped by You. You have good plans for my life, and I understand they don't involve living distracted. Holy Spirit, enlighten my mind and open my heart to what You desire for me to learn today. Teach me in Your love and grace, and please remove any distractions that might try to take my focus off You. Amen.*

Today and tomorrow, read Chapter 10 of *Right Now Matters*.

## INQUIRE

Sometimes we lose our focus, and some days we simply need to adjust our focus. Take a moment to discern honestly where your focus has been lately. Could it be time to refocus on what truly matters? Write down what comes to your mind here.

_____

_____

_____

_____

_____

## GIVE

Give yourself permission to refocus on what's important in your life. It's wise to give yourself time to refocus daily. Today's study will help do that.

## HEART

What we focus on matters. In Chapter 10 of *Right Now Matters,* I share the story of running hurdles in track and how my focus impacted my run that particular day. Interestingly, I recently found a newspaper clipping with a photo of me running the hurdles with my wrapped, skinned-up knee—likely from that very tumble from my misdirected focus. That was a difficult (but important) lesson for me to learn at a young age.

We will naturally follow our focus. I've heard Lysa TerKeurst, founder of Proverbs 31 Ministries, say, "We steer where we stare." Isn't that the truth, both generally in life and in overcoming distractions? For example, when my phone buzzes with a notification, that becomes my focus. That's not always necessarily a bad thing, but if it pulls me away from something or someone more important, that's not the best thing. Again, what we focus on we follow. I've been known to then get distracted by something else on my phone, and twenty minutes later, I find myself scrolling social media and responding to emails. Good grief! Our focus matters.

## TRUTH

God's Word has much to say about focus. Do a search and you'll find numerous Bible verses on the subject. I reference a couple in Chapter 10 of *Right Now Matters.* Today we are diving into a few of these. Open your Bible and locate each Scripture listed. Read them slowly, and either write them out or jot down the key words that stand out to you in each passage.

Colossians 3:2

_____

_____

_____

2 Corinthians 4:18

_____

_____

_____

Proverbs 4:25

_____

_____

_____

Romans 8:5

_____

_____

_____

Looking at the Colossians 3:2 verse a little further, The Message paraphrase states verses 1 and 2 this way: "So if you're serious about living this new resurrection life with Christ, _act_ like it. Pursue the things over which Christ presides. Don't shuffle along, eyes to the ground, absorbed with the things right in front of you. Look up, and be alert to what is going on around Christ—that's where the action is. See things from _his_ perspective." What

151

words stand out to you in this paraphrase? Write them here.

_____

_____

_____

_____

_____

The words that stand out to me are "serious, resurrection life, pursue, don't shuffle along, look up, be alert, action," and *"his* perspective."

What if we saw and lived life from His perspective? What if we focused on what He focuses on? That's a tall order, I realize, and I'm not sure we can fully and successfully do it. But with His equipping power, we can certainly have that be our focus. After all, it will only be in His power and in His strength that we can live this way. What do we have to lose?

## NEW

Our focus matters. What new thought or realization is God giving you regarding your focus as you read through the above verses? Write it down here.

_____

_____

_____

_____

_____

## OPEN

Colossians 3:2 in The Voice translation reminds us to "stay focused on what's above." Other translations reference "what's above" as "heavenly things." Take a few moments to ponder and brainstorm in the space below "what's above" and the "heavenly things" in your life. I give some suggestions in Chapter 10 of *Right Now Matters,* such as spiritual or faithful things, including love, joy, and peace. Write what you come up with here.

Heavenly things:

_____

_____

_____

_____

_____

That same verse says we aren't to focus on the "earthly things." Ponder and brainstorm the "earthly things" in your life. Write them out here.

Earthly things:

_____

_____

_____

_____

_____

Look at both lists. Honestly evaluate what you focus on more often. According to Colossians 3:2, are you doing well, focusing on "heavenly things"? Or do you focus on the "earthly things" more often? Write your realizations and thoughts on the following page.

_____

_____

_____

_____

## WALK

**Right-Now Women understand our focus matters.** Well done on completing Day 19. Now it's time to walk it out.

Write down what you learned from your study today, what you intend to apply to your life, and any adjustments God is leading you to make regarding your focus.

_____

_____

_____

_____

_____

Well done, Right-Now Woman!

Pray:

_Lord, thank You for this time and for teaching me truth. Help me to see and live this life from Your perspective. Help me to focus on the things on which You focus. Guide me to pursue the things over which You preside. Lead me to focus on what truly matters. Amen._

Use the space on the next page to journal any additional prayers, thoughts, or insights.

# DAY 20

*Right-Now Women keep our focus on
God, even if we do it imperfectly.*

---

**READY**

Take a slow, deep breath. Prepare your heart. Ask the Holy Spirit to enlighten your mind, remove distractions, and open your heart to what God has for you today.

Pray:

*Lord, thank You for how You meet me where I am and for loving me for who I am—who You created me to be. You know what I need before I need it, and You provide for all my needs. As I sit with You today, I ask You to provide what I need to learn and what You want me to apply to my life. Holy Spirit, help me to be undistracted during this time and open my heart to Your truth. Amen.*

Continue reading Chapter 10 of *Right Now Matters*.

**INQUIRE**

When we're distracted by the bigger stuff, we may not hear God's voice in the small stuff. What "big stuff" is grabbing your attention today? Could it be pulling you from God's still, small voice? Consider these questions, and write down your thoughts.

_____

_____

_____

_____

_____

## GIVE

Give yourself permission to listen for God's still, small voice in your life and circumstances today. Today's study will help to do that.

## HEART

We discussed yesterday the heavenly things as referenced in Colossians 3:2, which I also highlight in Chapter 10 of _Right Now Matters._ We looked at how Scripture encourages us to focus on those and not the earthly things. I don't know about you, but sometimes the earthly things snatch me away from the heavenly things. Sometimes those can be my biggest distractions in a day. Sadly, when I'm distracted by focusing on earthly things, I can easily miss the wonderful, heavenly things of which God may want to bless me. It's such a battle, isn't it?

In today's study, our focus is on the little gifts, truths, blessings, or words God might want to share with us as we look at the example of God and Elijah.

## TRUTH

Expanding on this account today, we read of how God met Elijah in the cave in 1 Kings 19:9-13. It's noted in Chapter 10 of _Right Now Matters,_ but open your Bible and read it for your own reference. Write down any words or phrases that stand out to you.

_____

_____

_____

_____

Sometimes when I think of God, I think of His power, majesty, authority, sovereignty, and almightiness. Those characteristics and attributes of God remind me of the big things like the great and powerful wind, or the earthquake, or the fire in this passage. God is bigger than our minds can contain, isn't He? He is all-knowing, all-powerful, all-consuming, and all-encompassing. I recall a children's song that tells of how big, strong, and mighty God is, and that there's nothing He cannot do.

But God wasn't in the powerful earthquake, wind, or fire when He met Elijah. Instead, He was found in the gentle whisper. I love the question God asked Elijah in both verses 9 and 13: "What are you doing here, Elijah?" Could God be asking us a similar question? What are we doing here? I asked this question in Chapter 10 of *Right Now Matters,* but I think it's worth repeating and answering here, too. What are you doing here? Take a moment to ponder this question, and write down anything God reveals to you.

_____

_____

_____

_____

_____

Sometimes the heavenly things are the small things. But we'll miss them every time if we're distracted with something else. Whether He reveals Himself to us in the big things of life or the small things, we won't miss God if we keep our eyes focused on Him. Our focus does matter.

Read through the examples of women in the Bible who lived undistracted and focused on God on pages 137 and 138 in *Right Now Matters.* I also invite you to read through the corresponding Bible references for the full perspective. Which woman's story and focus stands out to you the most? From that story, what's one thing you could apply to your life regarding your focus and living undistracted?

_____

_____

_____

_____

_____

## NEW

God invites us to live undistracted by keeping our focus on Him. Our focus matters because right now matters. What new insight or perspective is God revealing to you regarding your focus through today's study? Write it down here.

_____

_____

_____

_____

## OPEN

You and I have various responsibilities and commitments to focus on every day. These may include our work, our families, our relationships, our callings, and our convictions. On any given day, our focus plate is full. This exercise may help us keep it all in perspective.

On the next page is a target that represents our lives. I'm not a hunter, and

I rarely play darts, but we understand the purpose of a target, right? We always aim for the bullseye in the center. That's our focus. In this target, God is our bullseye. He's our focus, and we want to keep Him in that place. In the empty spaces beyond the target in the corners of the page, list as many things you can think of that you typically focus on in a day. Then plug those somewhere into the target, with the most crucial and important ones near the center circle—God's bullseye. Put the least important ones toward the outside of the target.

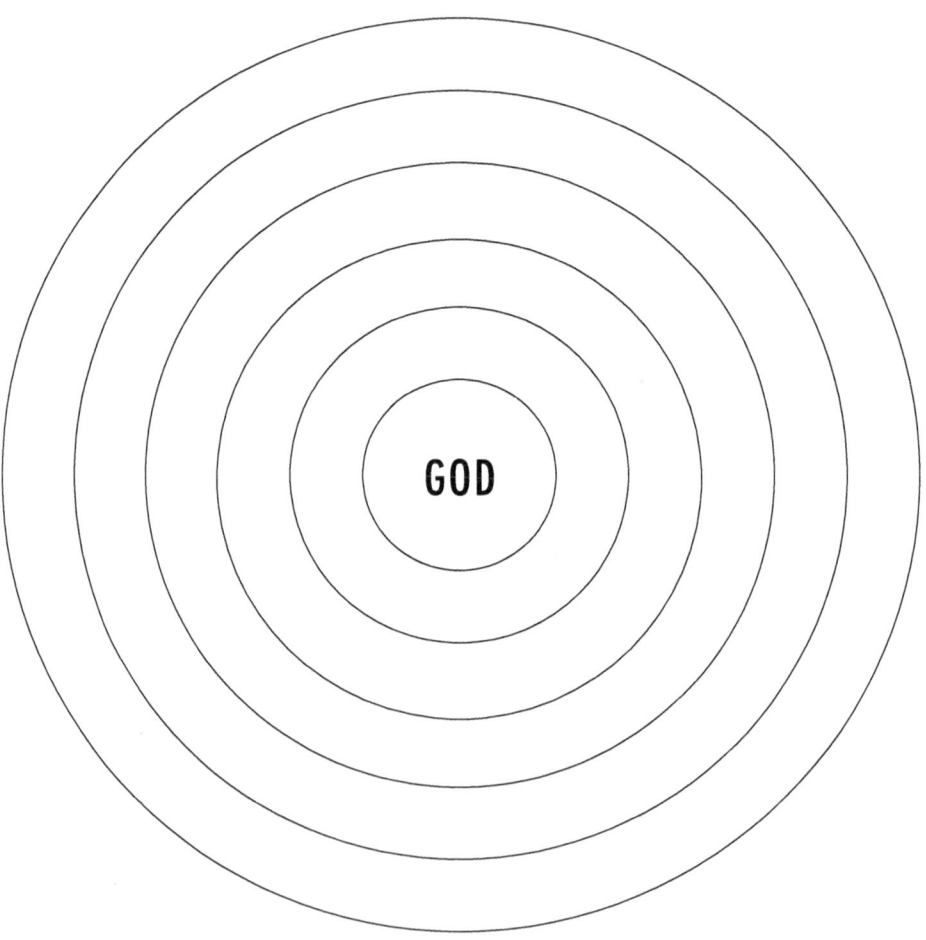

Seeing our reality in black and white sometimes helps us understand our current life and any adjustments we may need to make. As you look at your target and what's most important for you to focus on, do you feel more empowered and encouraged?

_____

_____

_____

_____

_____

What is God showing you through this exercise?

_____

_____

_____

_____

_____

Are you prompted to make any adjustments to your daily focus? If so, what?

_____

_____

_____

_____

_____

## WALK

**Right-Now Women keep our focus on God, even if we do it imperfectly.**
Well done on completing Day 20. Now it's time to walk it out.

Write down what you learned from your study today, what you intend to apply to your life, and any adjustments you want to make regarding where you set your focus.

_____

_____

_____

_____

_____

Well done, Right-Now Woman!

Pray:

_Lord, thank You for showing me what I'm currently focusing on and any areas I need to adjust. Please help me keep my focus on You, and equip me to always keep You in the center of my life. I know this matters. I love You. Amen._

Use the space on the next page to journal any additional prayers, thoughts, or insights.

# DAY 21

*Right-Now Women use diversions to aid us in daily life.*

---

## READY

Take a slow, deep breath. Prepare your heart. Ask the Holy Spirit to enlighten your mind, remove distractions, and open your heart to what God has for you today.

Pray:

*Thank You, Lord, for this time with You. It's a joy to spend time learning from You and sitting in Your presence. I invite the Holy Spirit here to enlighten my mind and to help me learn the truths You have for me today. Teach me and guide me in Your ways, O Lord. Please protect me from any distractions that could interrupt our time together. Amen.*

Today and tomorrow, read Chapter 11 of *Right Now Matters.*

## INQUIRE

We've discussed how distractions bring discouragement, destruction, and negativity to our lives. What about another view of distractions? Can distractions actually be good? And good for us? Give this some thought and share in the space below.

_____

_____

_____

_____

## GIVE

Give yourself permission to be open to the possibility that not all distractions are necessarily bad. Allow yourself to expand your thinking if this is a new thought for you.

## HEART

In Chapter 11 of *Right Now Matters,* I label "good distractions" as diversions. Diversions help shift our focus and divert our attention away to something else. The example I'm thinking of right now is regarding the bag of my favorite kind of chips in our kitchen pantry. Why? Because I'm craving them right now. Instead of giving in to them, however, I'm choosing to divert my attention to eating an apple. I'm hoping the crunchiness of an apple will replace my desire for the crunch of the chips. The apple is my diversion. Let's hope it works.

The apple is a better choice for me than chips, and that's how I view diversions. They are better choices for me than distractions. I share in Chapter 11 of *Right Now Matters* how the "why" matters regarding this. When we ask ourselves why we are being distracted, the answer reveals the issue. *Is this pulling me away from my life, or is it making my life better?* The apple is making my life better.

Sometimes we can proactively choose healthy diversions like I'm doing right now. I share a list of helpful diversions on pages 148 and 149 in *Right Now Matters.* Other times we may be forced to quickly decide between choosing a distraction or a diversion. Which one will we choose?

What about you? Do you use any diversions in your life? These are things that may seem like distractions but are making your life better, instead. Think about this for a moment, and list any that come to your mind here.

_____

_____

_____

_____

_____

## TRUTH

I share practical ideas and ways to incorporate diversions into our lives in Chapter 11 of *Right Now Matters.* But what does God say about this? If diversions help us cope, positively redirect, and release stress and anxiety, this is about caring for ourselves. It's important to seek God in this, as He has much to say about it in His Word. Open your Bible, and read the following three Scripture verses. Write them out so you can remember them later, and then answer the question below each one.

1 Peter 5:7

_____

_____

_____

We pondered this verse in our Day 11 study, but this truth is important. Giving our anxiety to God is a helpful diversion. What anxiety can you cast (hurl, throw) to God today?

_____

_____

_____

_____

_____

Matthew 6:33

_____

_____

_____

Seeking God first is a helpful diversion. In what ways can you seek first God's kingdom (rule, authority) and righteousness (faithfulness, truthfulness)?

_____

_____

_____

_____

_____

Romans 12:2

_____

_____

_____

_____

Renewing our minds is a helpful diversion. What will help you renew your mind today?

_____

_____

_____

_____

_____

God may not clearly speak about helpful diversions in His Word, but He certainly emphasizes caring for ourselves. Using helpful diversions can equip us to do that.

## NEW

Right now matters, and the diversions both God and we use matters. How is God growing your thinking about these helpful tools—diversions— through today's study? What is He revealing to you about them in your life? Write it out here.

_____

_____

_____

_____

_____

_____

## OPEN

Use the space on the next page to look at distractions and diversions a little closer. This may help define these better using real-life examples. Following the provided examples, add those that apply to you and your life. List a distraction in the DISTRACTION column, and then a diversion in the DIVERSION column that can help redirect.

| Distraction: | Diversion: |
|---|---|
| Overwhelming thoughts | Taking a walk to clear my mind and pray |
| Anxiety about an upcoming event | Praying about the anxiety |
| A stressful situation | Taking deep breaths and relaxing |

After this exercise, can you now see the value of using diversions in your life?

## WALK

**Right-Now Women use diversions to aid us in daily life.** Great job completing Day 21. It's time to walk it out.

Write down what you learned today, what you intend to apply to your life, and which diversions appeal to you or apply to you the most in your current circumstances.

_____

_____

_____

_____

_____

Well done, Right-Now Woman!

Pray:

*Lord, thank You for expanding my thinking and helping me to understand how diversions can be helpful in my life. Will You please show me which ones are best for me and my current circumstances, and will You help me use them in helpful and positive ways? Thank You for Your consistent love and care for me. Amen.*

Use the space on the next page to journal any additional prayers, thoughts, or insights.

# DAY 22

*Right-Now Women recognize God may use
diversions to guide us on His perfect path.*

---

## READY

Take a slow, deep breath. Prepare your heart. Ask the Holy Spirit to enlighten your mind, remove distractions, and open your heart to what God has for you today.

Pray:

*Lord, You always have Your best in mind for me, and I thank You for that. You continue to guide me and mold me into the woman You desire me to be. I am so grateful. Prepare my heart for what You have for me today, and Holy Spirit, please lead me and help me understand Your truth. Guard me from any distracting thoughts or interruptions during our time together. Amen.*

Continue reading Chapter 11 of *Right Now Matters*.

## INQUIRE

Scan back over your life for a few moments. When has God used diversions in your life for good? How did He do so, and what did He do? What good came from them? Share any details here.

_____

_____

_____

_____

## GIVE

Give yourself permission to open yourself and your well-laid plans to God for His plans and purposes instead. Be willing to accept any diversions He may be using now or will use in the future.

## HEART

God always knows what's best for us, but sometimes in the moment we're perplexed because we don't understand. We can't see what He's doing, nor can we know. When we aren't aware of His plans, we question and wonder—especially when those plans catch us off guard.

I share in Chapter 11 of *Right Now Matters* two stories about my daughter and how God used what we thought were distractions at the time as helpful diversions in her life. God orchestrated events and situations behind the scenes that we weren't aware of to guide her in the directions He wanted her to go. It was uncomfortable for Alissa at the time—and confusing. But God led her one step at a time in these diversions to the point she was able to see He had different plans for her life than she did.

Could God be using diversions in your life today? Could He be guiding you in a different direction than the one you're currently heading? Write down any thoughts here.

_____

_____

_____

_____

_____

_____

## TRUTH

God used diversions in the lives of those in the Bible, too. Open your Bible to Acts 16. Paul documented two instances of God diverting Paul and his companions as they traveled. Read verses 6-10. Write down the diversions and any additional details you notice.

1. _____

_____

_____

_____

2. _____

_____

_____

_____

What, instead, were God's plans for Paul and his traveling companions? How did He reveal them to Paul?

_____

_____

_____

_____

_____

_____

God's plans are much better than ours, and thankfully, He loves us enough to divert us in the direction that's best for us—His best for us.

What about other examples of God's diversions in the Bible? There's Joseph. God diverted him to Egypt by the not-so-scenic route to save many lives from starvation. Remember Moses? God took him from a life of luxury to eventually lead His people to the Promised Land. This might be the greatest diversion of all: Mary and Joseph. God chose this unlikely couple to give birth to and raise the Savior of the world, Jesus. God had bigger plans for these people than they ever could have imagined or guessed!

He has plans for us, too—plans that are greater than we can even dream. May we allow God to divert us in His perfect ways, for our growth, for the good of others, and for His glory.

## NEW

God can use whatever He wants to divert us to receive His best. What new thoughts is God giving you regarding diversions through today's study? What is He revealing to you? Write it out here.

_____

_____

_____

_____

_____

## OPEN

We don't know the ways of God, and we aren't aware of His plans for us. We can't begin to outguess God. To encourage your heart today, write down any disappointment, roadblock, bad news received, or difficult situation you're currently experiencing.

_____

_____

_____

_____

_____

_____

_____

_____

_____

_____

_____

_____

We become encouraged and hopeful when we look beyond these situations and circumstances to how God might be using them for good. God could be using these as diversions to bring about His perfect plans and purposes for your life.

Imagine handing to God each one of the situations and circumstances you wrote down. Offer them to Him, and surrender them to His care. Then take heart, and let God do what only He can do in and through them. Allow God to encourage you through this exercise.

## WALK

**Right-Now Women recognize God may use diversions to guide us on His perfect path.** Great job completing Day 22. It's time to walk it out.

Write down what you learned today, what you intend to apply to your life, and how your perspective has changed regarding diversions.

_____

_____

_____

_____

_____

Well done, Right-Now Woman!

Pray:

*Father God, thank You for helping me see that not all distractions are bad, and how sometimes You use diversions for our growth, for the good of others, and for Your glory. I am grateful You love and care enough about me that You continue to guide me on the path that's best for me. Thank You. In the days to come, help me recognize diversions and how You may be using them in my life. I love You. Amen.*

Use the space on the next page to journal any additional prayers, thoughts, or insights.

# DAY 23

*Right-Now Women focus on living lives of love.*

## READY

Take a slow, deep breath. Prepare your heart. Ask the Holy Spirit to enlighten your mind, remove distractions, and open your heart to what God has for you today.

Pray:

*Lord, I look back at the progress we've made together through this study, and I am grateful. I pause today to thank You and praise You. You continue to help me see there's a more abundant way to live with You. Holy Spirit, guide me to Your truth, and lead me in this study today. Remove any distractions from my presence. Amen.*

Today and tomorrow, read Chapter 12 of *Right Now Matters*.

## INQUIRE

Take a moment to think about the special people in your life—your family, friends, coworkers, neighbors, acquaintances, members of groups of which you belong. Try to recall the last time you spent time or talked with them. Were you fully present on each occasion? As you recall, were you distracted in any way? Write what you remember here.

_____

_____

_____

_____

_____

_____

## GIVE

Give yourself permission to evaluate how present you are in your relation-ships and to make any necessary changes that God prompts.

## HEART

Living undistracted and in the right now isn't always just about us. Sure, it's important for us to live in the moment to be effective and impactful and to not miss the blessings God has for us, but it's also important to live in the moment for the benefit of others. It takes on an entirely different meaning when living in the right now motivates us to love, serve, and bless other people. Could the bigger gift in living undistracted be the giving of our full selves to those in our lives?

When we intentionally live in the present, we are better equipped to con-nect with and respond to those around us. Whether they are in our homes, our offices, our neighborhoods, or receiving our emails or texts, we are more available to notice occasions to bless and assist. We are better able to be attentive to the needs and joys of others, and we will build stronger relationships with them because of our live-in-the-moment presence. This truly matters.

For example, take the story I shared in the Introduction of _Right Now Mat-ters._ If I had stayed present during my son's soccer game, not only would I not have missed his goal, but I would have also been able to be a blessing to those around me in the stands. I would have been able to impact others for good—and for God—that evening.

## TRUTH

The people in our lives need us to be present. I'm not the best at staying present in my own strength. I do much better when I rely on God's strength and ask Him to help me.

Several Scriptures in the Bible encourage us to do all we can to build healthy and vibrant relationships with one another. We can't do that when we're distracted. One verse stands out to me regarding this, and it's the foundation for all we do in our Christian faith. It contains four simple—yet incredibly profound—words. Let's look at it together. Open your Bible to 1 Corinthians 16:14. Here it is in the NIV translation: "Do everything in love."

Pause a moment, and allow that to sink in.

This means *everything.* Everything. Not just when I feel like it, or not just when it's easy. It's also not dependent on the situation, the task, or on another's behavior. It's *everything.*

Staying fully present with those we do life with is a way of doing "everything in love." It honors them, it blesses them, and it strengthens our relationships with them. As a result, they feel loved, appreciated, and valued.

Here are a few more verses that support this. Read these, and write them down to recall later.

Romans 12:10

_____

_____

_____

_____

_____

Philippians 2:3-4

_____

_____

_____

_____

_____

Matthew 7:12

_____

_____

_____

_____

Which one inspires you the most to show love to others by living undistracted and staying present? Why?

_____

_____

_____

_____

_____

_____

## NEW

People in our lives deserve our full presence and attention. What new thought or realization is God impressing upon you as you understand living undistracted isn't just about us? Write it down here.

_____

_____

_____

_____

_____

## OPEN

As we ponder the 1 Corinthians 14:16 verse to "do everything in love," it's easy to read and recite but maybe not so easy to live out daily. Living undistracted helps us love others and treat them the way they deserve.

Let's put this in perspective. Think of all the things you do with or regarding others, and use these to fill in the blanks below. Replace the "do everything" with a tangible way to show love. Here's an example. Instead of "Do everything in love," one might be, "Take out the trash for my husband in love." Give it a try, and be willing to get creative.

_____ in love.

_____ in love.

_____ in love.

_____ in love.

_____ in love.

_____ in love.

_____ in love.

_____ in love.

_____ in love.

_____ in love.

_____ in love.

_____ in love.

When we see these opportunities in black and white, we are more motivated to do all we can in love. Everything. Which one motivates you the most right now?

_____

_____

_____

_____

_____

We will look at this further in tomorrow's study.

## WALK

**Right-Now Women focus on living lives of love.** Congratulations on completing Day 23. Now it's time to walk it out.

Write down what you learned from your study today, what you intend to apply to your life, and one practical way you can show love to others this week by living undistracted and staying present.

_____

_____

_____

_____

_____

Well done, Right-Now Woman!

Pray:

_Thank You, God, for reminding me how important it is to live a life of love and to show love to others by staying fully present with them. I understand now how this is a tangible and intentional way to make others a priority. Please help me to do this well, and show me how to continually love others by living undistracted. Amen._

Use the space on the next page to journal any additional prayers, thoughts, or insights.

# DAY 24

*Right-Now Women desire to bless
others as we live undistracted.*

## READY

Take a slow, deep breath. Prepare your heart. Ask the Holy Spirit to enlighten your mind, remove distractions, and open your heart to what God has for you today.

Pray:

*Thank You, God, for giving me this opportunity to spend time with You. I cherish these moments with You in Your Word, in prayer, and in Your presence. Please, will You continue to lead me into Your truth today? Holy Spirit, equip me to comprehend and apply that truth. Remove any distraction that might try to take my focus off You during this time. Thank You. Amen.*

Continue reading Chapter 12 of *Right Now Matters*.

## INQUIRE

Yesterday we reflected on staying present in our relationships and how important that is to us and to those in our lives. Is there a person in your life who does this well? Take a moment to ponder this question, and name the person in the space below. Also write down what you notice and appreciate about this person remaining fully present with others.

_____

_____

_____

_____

_____

## GIVE

Give yourself permission to use another person as an example to follow in living undistracted and staying fully present in the moment while you're with others.

## HEART

We've already studied how Jesus was the master at living undistracted. He modeled staying present well. 1 share some examples in Chapter 12 of *Right Now Matters:* feeding the five thousand, as the children came to Him, when He reclined with His disciples at the Last Supper, when He noticed others, and as He carried His cross to Calvary.

If anyone had a reason to live distracted, 1 would say it was Jesus. He had countless people vying for His attention, was under great persecution, had multitudes following Him, and knew the cross was waiting for Him. That's a lot to be distracted by, isn't it? All of this would certainly distract me. Goodness, 1 get distracted by far lesser issues!

Jesus stayed present. We never see in Scripture any indication of distracted living on His part. He was always living in the moment, always present, always doing the work of the Father—even when it wasn't convenient. Even when it wasn't easy. Even while He was on the road to His death. 1 want to be more like Jesus, don't you?

## TRUTH

Looking through Scripture, we see example after example of how Jesus lived undistracted. He put others first yet didn't sacrifice time with His Father to do so. He knew where His strength came from, and we know where ours comes from, too, don't we? We discussed this earlier in our study. Jesus stayed present for the people who needed Him and for those whose lives would be impacted for all eternity through Him.

Of all the accounts in Scripture, I would guess one of the biggest occasions for Jesus to be distracted is found in Matthew 4:1-11 when He was tempted by the devil. Open your Bible, and read the passage. List the ways the devil tempted Him and Jesus' response to each temptation.

**devil's temptation:**                    **Jesus' response:**

Two facts stand out to me in the first two verses: 1) the Spirit led Jesus into the wilderness to be tempted, and 2) after fasting forty days and nights, He was hungry. This encounter was intentional by the Spirit. Jesus didn't just happen upon the devil one day. No, He was deliberately led there to be tempted, and Jesus responded purposefully, even though physically He was hungry. I don't know about you, but when I get hungry, I can get very distracted. Yet Jesus had just fasted forty days and nights. He might have been physically hungry, but I'm thinking He was spiritually fed and strong because of the fasting. If you've ever practiced this spiritual discipline, you might understand what I mean.

Another occasion when Jesus could have been distracted—but wasn't—was one I mention in Chapter 12 of *Right Now Matters* regarding the woman who touched His cloak in the crowd. It's found in Luke 8:43-48. Locate that passage, and read it. List what you notice here.

_____

_____

_____

_____

_____

The crowd was pressing against Jesus, yet Jesus felt power go out from Him when the bleeding woman touched the edge of His clothes. He noticed, stopped, addressed her, and affirmed her faith. "Daughter, your faith has healed you. Go in peace" (Luke 8:48).

What other accounts in the Bible come to your mind when Jesus could have been distracted, but wasn't?

_____

_____

_____

_____

_____

What was His secret? How did He stay fully present and undistracted? Could it be because He was spiritually strong by spending time with His Father? Or because He was in tune with His Father's plans in each moment He was living? How can we do this?

_____

_____

_____

_____

_____

## NEW

We may not be Jesus, but we can follow His example in staying fully present for the sake of others. What new thought or hope is God showing you today through this study? Write it here.

_____

_____

_____

_____

## OPEN

I include the last poem I ever wrote at the end of Chapter 12 of *Right Now Matters*. Before I wrote it, I remember listing all the ways I wanted to be a blessing to others. This was before I began this journey of living undistracted, but even back then my desire was to bless others.

Read through my simple poem again. In your own words, write down how you want to be a blessing to others as you live undistracted. Then take your words or phrases and form them into your own poem. It doesn't have to be elaborate or fancy, but just let the words flow. Allow yourself to get creative, and have fun with this exercise.

How I want to bless others by living undistracted:

_____

_____

_____

_____

_____

My poem:

_____

_____

_____

_____

_____

_____

_____

_____

Go back and read your poem, and celebrate this moment. Right now matters.

## WALK

**Right-Now Women desire to bless others as we live undistracted.** Congratulations on completing Day 24. Now it's time to walk it out.

Write down what you learned from your study today, what you intend to apply to your life, and how you can follow Jesus' example in staying fully present with others.

_____

_____

_____

_____

_____

Well done, Right-Now Woman!

Pray:

*Lord God, the examples of Jesus in Scripture inspire me so. Please help me to live an undistracted life like He did, in Your power and in Your strength. Thank You for continuing to mold me into the woman You desire me to be. Amen.*

To access the printable form of my poem, *Lord, Help Me Be a Blessing Today* in Chapter 12 of *Right Now Matters,* turn to the Appendix.

Use the space on the next page to journal any additional prayers, thoughts, or insights.

# DAY 25

*Right-Now Women understand
the importance of prayer.*

## READY

Take a slow, deep breath. Prepare your heart. Ask the Holy Spirit to enlighten your mind, remove distractions, and open your heart to what God has for you today.

Pray:

*Your ways and thoughts are far above mine, God, and I thank You for how You have good plans for my life. As I spend time with You today in Your Word and in prayer, please continue to teach me and guide me. Holy Spirit, capture my attention and enlighten my mind. Help me to ignore any distractions that try to entice me away. Amen.*

Today and tomorrow, read Chapter 13 of *Right Now Matters*.

## INQUIRE

What does your prayer life look like? This is not to make you feel superior or inferior; it's just a simple question to ponder and answer. Go ahead and give this some thought, then describe your prayer life in the space below.

_____

_____

_____

_____

## GIVE

Give yourself permission today to be open to prayer and to ways to grow your prayer life.

## HEART

Prayer is simply talking with God, and it's the primary way we communicate and connect with Him. I used to think prayer had to be done a certain way, and that I needed to recite certain words to talk to God. At another point in my life, I thought prayer had to be a big production, with a certain space and in solitude and quiet. I soon learned I could pray anywhere, with or without anyone, and I could just have a conversation with God—like I would with anyone else.

Every day on Instagram I currently share "Today's Simple Prayer." In less than ten seconds, I offer an uncomplicated prayer with a background of a sunrise, a sunset, or a beach scene I captured. I do this to remind myself and others that prayer doesn't have to be complicated. We can keep prayer simple and authentic. May these short, simple prayers be springboards for others to use in their own prayer lives. Why do we make it more complicated than it needs to be?

God just wants us to communicate and spend time with Him. Period. We can simply be ourselves and talk to Him like we talk to a friend or family member. Prayer is a beautiful gift!

## TRUTH

When I first began praying, I really didn't know what to pray. My prayers were typically one-sided, with my wants, my needs, my hopes, and my dreams. Someone encouraged me to begin praying Scripture, and doing so completely changed my prayer life. Not only that, but it also deepened my faith as I began to learn Scripture simultaneously.

Below are some Bible verses I pray often. They either read as a prayer as written in the Bible, or I form them into one. Open your Bible and locate them. Write them out in the space beside each one, and then read them as prayers.

Psalm 25:4-5

_____

_____

_____

_____

_____

Psalm 51:10

_____

_____

_____

_____

Psalm 56:3

_____

_____

_____

_____

Psalm 139:13-14

_____

_____

_____

_____

_____

Isaiah 25:1

_____

_____

_____

_____

_____

Revelation 4:11

_____

_____

_____

_____

_____

Which one touches your heart the most? Why?

_____

_____

_____

_____

_____

What other Scriptures can you pray? Spend some time thumbing through your Bible to find more. Write out these verses here for future reference.

_____

_____

_____

_____

_____

_____

_____

## NEW

Prayer is powerful, and it's a way to communicate and connect with our Creator. What new thought or realization is God showing you regarding prayer? Write it down here.

_____

_____

_____

_____

_____

## OPEN

What stops you or prevents you from praying? Take a few moments to list these distractions. Then next to them write what you can proactively do to alleviate them. Write down as many as you can. I've given you an example.

**Distraction:**                    **Diversion:**

My phone                            Put phone away

Now that you have a list of prayer distractions and ways to overcome them, you are better equipped to enjoy your prayer time—distraction-free.

## WALK

**Right-Now Women understand the importance of prayer.** Congratulations on completing Day 25. Now it's time to walk it out.

Write down what you learned from your study today, what you intend to apply to your life, and how you plan to either incorporate Scripture into your prayers or be proactive regarding distractions in your prayer time.

_____

_____

_____

_____

_____

Well done, Right-Now Woman!

Pray:

*God, thank You for helping me learn how to better communicate and connect with You through prayer. You know where I struggle with this, and You understand my tendencies. Please help me to talk to You throughout the day as I would a friend. I look forward to growing closer to You through prayer in the days to come. Amen.*

Use the space on the next page to journal any additional prayers, thoughts, or insights.

# DAY 26

*Right-Now Women work as we pray
and pray while we work.*

## READY

Take a slow, deep breath. Prepare your heart. Ask the Holy Spirit to enlighten your mind, remove distractions, and open your heart to what God has for you today.

Pray:

*Father God, I praise You for who You are and all You are. Thank You for loving me enough to not leave me as I once was but to continue to help me be more like Your Son, Jesus. Holy Spirit, please teach me today, and help me grasp what You have for me to learn. Help me stay undistracted in these moments with You. Amen.*

Continue reading Chapter 13 of *Right Now Matters.*

## INQUIRE

You have commitments and responsibilities each day. Some of these might make you feel overwhelmed and your schedule to appear overloaded. Like I do, I'm guessing you sometimes face difficult circumstances and situations that are beyond your control. What do you do when life feels out of control? Do you attempt to handle everything yourself, or do you seek God in these times? Take a moment to answer here.

_____

_____

_____

_____

_____

## GIVE

Give yourself permission today to seek God in prayer *first* for all you need in every area of your life.

## HEART

When trials or opposition emerge in my life, 1 often think of the story of Nehemiah in the Bible. 1 share some of it in Chapter 13 of *Right Now Matters*. God used Nehemiah, an ordinary man, a cupbearer of the king of Persia, in an extraordinary way—to rebuild Jerusalem's wall. The text doesn't indicate he was trained as a builder or as a leader, but that didn't stop God from using him, and that didn't stop Nehemiah from stepping into unknown and unfamiliar territory. Nehemiah knew his God, including His character and His faithfulness. He also trusted God would provide all he needed to complete his calling and this task. He partnered with God in prayer for strength, help, and guidance. Nehemiah knew he couldn't complete this mission without God's presence and power.

What about you, and what about me? Do we know God, His character, and His faithfulness? Do we partner with God in prayer and trust Him to provide all we need?

## TRUTH

Let's look at this a little deeper because God's words are far better than mine. Open your Bible to Nehemiah 2. Today's reading is the longest portion of this study, but 1 promise, it will be worth it. Read the full account of Nehemiah rebuilding Jerusalem's wall in Nehemiah Chapters 2-6. Take your time, and in the space below, note the many times Nehemiah prayed.

_____

_____

_____

_____

_____

Do any of these instances stand out to you? Put an asterisk by those that do. One thing that is prominent to me happens right away in verse 4 of Chapter 2. Nehemiah was already praying "to the God of heaven." Nehemiah was clearly a praying man. He invited God into every circumstance and situation through prayer. God heard Nehemiah's prayers and the prayers of the people and acted on their behalf. Nehemiah was an example for others regarding prayer—so much so, even their enemies knew God helped Nehemiah and the others build this wall (Nehemiah 6:16).

Just think how different this account could read if Nehemiah wasn't a man of prayer and if he didn't turn to God for everything. Do you think the wall would have been finished in fifty-two days? I wonder.

We can appreciate how the people simultaneously built the wall and prepared themselves to fight off enemies' attacks with a trowel in one hand and a sword in the other. As I mention in Chapter 13 of *Right Now Matters,* this is an example for us. Our sword is prayer. We work and we pray simultaneously, too. Just like Nehemiah experienced, we receive God's power to do the work God calls us to when we use our sword—prayer.

## NEW

We work, and we pray. We pray as we work. What new thought or idea is

God revealing to you regarding Nehemiah's example and working and praying simultaneously? Write it down here.

_____

_____

_____

_____

## OPEN

Take a moment to ponder your current circumstances. What's your biggest opposition right now? What's your most threatening fear? What task feels largely ominous and beyond your capabilities? Open your heart to God, and write out a prayer to Him that addresses this in the space below. Give it all to Him, and lay it in His hands.

_____

_____

_____

_____

_____

_____

_____

Read through it, and pray it again. Come back to it whenever you need to, or use it as a model for future prayers.

## WALK

**Right-Now Women work as we pray, and pray while we work.** Congratulations on completing Day 26. Now it's time to walk it out.

Write down what you learned from your study today, what you intend to apply to your life, and how you can practically follow Nehemiah's example.

_____

_____

_____

_____

_____

Well done, Right-Now Woman!

Pray:

_Thank You, God, for helping me see how important prayer is in my life, and how important it is to You. It's a wonderful way I can partner with You in every situation and circumstance. Remind me to turn to You for and in everything. I give You glory and praise for this today. Amen._

To guide you further, find the ten Right Now Matters Scripture and Prayer Cards found in the Appendix.

Use the space on the next page to journal any additional prayers, thoughts, or insights.

# DAY 27

*Right-Now Women know who we are
in Christ and remember this often.*

### READY

Take a slow, deep breath. Prepare your heart. Ask the Holy Spirit to enlighten your mind, remove distractions, and open your heart to what God has for you today.

Pray:

*Lord, I praise You for how You care for me and provide what I need when I need it. You continue to teach me and guide me, and I thank You for that. Please lead me in Your ways as I spend this time with You today. Holy Spirit, help me to understand and to apply what You show me. Keep all distractions away as I spend this time with You. Amen.*

Today and tomorrow, read Chapter 14 of *Right Now Matters.*

### INQUIRE

Who do you say you are? When you think about yourself, what words come to mind? God already knows, but sometimes it's good for us to see on paper exactly what we think and say about ourselves. Take a moment to ponder these questions, and answer them honestly in the space below.

_____

_____

_____

_____

_____

## GIVE

Give yourself permission today to see yourself through God's eyes and through a fresh perspective.

## HEART

God created you magnificently and wonderfully. He knows you better than you know yourself. He knew when He formed you in your mother's womb that you would be reading these very words today. He's so intimate and personal, and He loves you more than you can comprehend.

Thankfully, He doesn't leave us as we are—or as we once were. He draws us closer to Himself through our faith and changes us from the inside out. Think about this: every time you and I spend time with Him, we are changed because we are in the presence of the Living God. That simply makes my heart soar!

The other day I caught myself saying something extremely negative about myself. I knew as the words left my mouth, they weren't truth. Hearing what I voiced about myself caused me to feel something I would describe as a dart to my heart. It stung! What we say about and how we see ourselves matters. Not just a little, but a lot. It matters because God created us amazingly, and anything we think or say short of this is a lie.

For us to live as Right-Now Women, it's wise for us to embrace the truth of who we really are in God's eyes—not in the world's eyes or our own eyes. This will equip us to better live out this new way of life as a Right-Now Woman.

## TRUTH

God's Word has a great deal to say about who we are and how God created us. We don't read our Bibles to help us feel better about ourselves necessarily, but we cling to how they remind us of truth and of who God created us to be. Below are some Scriptures to help us focus on this. Open your Bible, and look up each Bible passage. Write the verses down in the spaces provided, and allow God to fill your heart and mind with His truth about you.

You are wonderfully made.

Psalm 139:13-16

_____

_____

_____

_____

_____

_____

You are made in God's image.

Genesis 1:26-27

_____

_____

_____

_____

_____

_____

You are a child of God.

John 1:12

_____

_____

_____

_____

_____

You are a temple of the Holy Spirit.

1 Corinthians 6:19

_____

_____

_____

_____

_____

You are a new creation in Christ.

2 Corinthians 5:17

_____

_____

_____

_____

You have been set free in Christ.

Galatians 5:1

_____

_____

_____

_____

_____


You are chosen, holy, and blameless before God.

Ephesians 1:4

_____

_____

_____

_____

_____


You are redeemed and forgiven through God's grace.

Ephesians 1:7

_____

_____

_____

_____

You are God's handiwork, created to do good works.

Ephesians 2:10

_____

_____

_____

_____

You are loved and chosen by God.

1 Thessalonians 1:4

_____

_____

_____

_____

Which of these truths touch your heart the most? Put an asterisk next to the ones that do. Return to this list whenever you need a reminder.

## NEW

Our identity in Christ matters, and it's important to remember it daily. What new thought or revelation is God impressing upon you regarding who you are in Him? Write it down here.

_____

_____

_____

_____

_____

## OPEN

Below are scrambled words from the Truth section above. Unscramble them in the space next to each word and claim them for who you are. (Answer key is on page 236.)

velod _____

hcnose _____

kaiwnhodr _____

ederemed _____

ngofriev _____

slbaeseml _____

loyh _____

ets refe _____

ewn erictano _____

etmlep _____

hcdli fo odG _____

dowefluynrl dame _____

soGd geami _____

## WALK

**Right-Now Women know who we are in Christ and remember this often.**
Congratulations on completing Day 27. Now it's time to walk it out.

Write down what you learned from your study today, what you intend to apply to your life, and how you can live in the truth of who God says you are.

_____

_____

_____

_____

_____

Well done, Right-Now Woman!

Pray:

*God, I thank You for the reminder of who I am in You because sometimes I forget. Sometimes I get distracted from this truth and get stuck in what's untrue. In the days to come, help me to remember what You've taught me today. Amen.*

Use the space on the next page to journal any additional prayers, thoughts, or insights.

# DAY 28

*Right-Now Women realize right now matters.*

---

## READY

Take a slow, deep breath. Prepare your heart. Ask the Holy Spirit to enlighten your mind, remove distractions, and open your heart to what God has for you today.

Pray:

*Thank You, God, for Your consistent guiding presence in my life and for guiding me through each day of this study. Holy Spirit, enlighten my mind and reveal to me Your truth. Please help me to focus on You during this time and remove any distractions. I desire to learn all You have for me. Amen.*

Continue reading Chapter 14 of *Right Now Matters.*

## INQUIRE

When you think of a Right-Now Woman, the term I refer to in Chapter 14 of *Right Now Matters,* what are the words that come to your mind? How would you describe yourself as a Right-Now Woman? Write down your thoughts here.

---

---

---

---

## GIVE

Give yourself permission today to see yourself as a Right-Now Woman.

## HEART

Who is a Right-Now Woman? She's a woman who trusts God, relies on Him for everything, and understands that living undistracted is imperative for embracing an abundant and fruitful life with Him. She fully comprehends how right now matters.

For the past twenty-seven days we've looked at how right now matters. We've dug deep into Scripture and asked God to speak to us through His Word—to change us and mold us into the women He desires us to be. We've contemplated our lives, answered some tough questions, and have faced uncomfortable realities. We've allowed the Holy Spirit to guide our thinking and to lead us into truth. And we've embraced a new, exciting, and freeing way to live these abundant lives God has given us. We are focused on living undistracted for our growth, for the good of others, and for God's glory.

We are Right-Now Women.

Let me be clear, however: we don't have it all figured out yet. That likely won't happen this side of eternity. God's the only One who has the full plans of this life. He's the One who knows all, sees all, and is in charge of all. But we are Right-Now Women because we fully know this is the only way to live—in the right now. We are Right-Now Women because right now matters.

## TRUTH

In Chapter 14 of *Right Now Matters,* we read about the woman described in Proverbs 31. The chapter includes twenty-one verses detailing the life of this blessed-by-God woman. Let's look at this account today. Open your Bible to Proverbs 31:10-31. Take your time reading it, even if you've read through it numerous times before. Ask God to reveal to you what He wants you to glean from this passage. In the space below, write down any words, phrases, or sentences that stand out to you.

_____

_____

_____

_____

_____

Which verse encourages you the most? Why?

_____

_____

_____

_____

Which verse challenges you the most? Why?

_____

_____

_____

_____

_____

Which verse motivates you to celebrate the woman you are in God today?

_____

_____

_____

_____

_____

As Lysa TerKeurst's quote in Chapter 14 of *Right Now Matters* reminds us, this passage isn't calling us to do more or be more, but to celebrate who we are. We are women of strength, valor, courage, and dignity in God's eyes. And as verse 25 declares, ". . .she smiles *when she thinks* about the future (Proverbs 31:25 Voice). As Right-Now Women, we can smile when we think about the future because of the hope we have and the abundant life we are living—all thanks to Jesus.

## NEW

We are now empowered to embrace a new lifestyle as Right-Now Women. What new thought or conviction is God giving you as you step into this new way of right-now living? Write it out here.

_____

_____

_____

_____

_____

## OPEN

Here's your opportunity to look back over these twenty-eight days and apply what you've learned. If you need a reminder, read through the Right-Now Women Life Declarations on pages 188 and 189 of *Right Now Matters*. You can find the printable access in the Appendix. Take some time, and answer these questions regarding how you will carry with you into the future the truths and promises you've learned through this study.

This impacted me the most:

_____

_____

_____

_____

_____

I wasn't aware I was living this way:

_____

_____

_____

_____

_____

The biggest change God is prompting me to make:

_____

_____

_____

_____

_____

This makes me uncomfortable regarding the days to come:

_____

_____

_____

_____

A truth God spoke to me:

_____

_____

_____

_____

The Bible verse that helped me the most:

_____

_____

_____

_____

_____

What I think will be the most difficult part in living as a Right-Now Woman:

_____

_____

_____

_____

I want to tell these women in my life about this study and my experience:

_____

_____

_____

_____

What I want to leave in the past:

_____

_____

_____

_____

My hopes for the future include:

_____

_____

_____

_____

_____

What I will now do when distractions try to pull me away:

_____

_____

_____

_____

_____

Through this study my relationship with God has changed in this way:

_____

_____

_____

_____

_____

## WALK

**Right-Now Women realize right now matters.** Congratulations on completing Day 28. Now it's time to walk it out.

Write down what you learned from your study today, what you intend to apply to your life, and how you will walk out your calling as a Right-Now Woman.

_____

_____

_____

_____

_____

Well done, Right-Now Woman!

Pray:

*Wow, thank You God for this journey. Thank You for helping me become a Right-Now Woman through Your guidance, strength, courage, and love. Thank You for not leaving me where I once was—lost in distractions—and for lifting my sights to a better, more fruitful, and abundant way to live. I am eternally grateful. Please continue to equip me in the days ahead. I love You. Amen.*

In the Appendix you can access the printable copy of the Right-Now Woman Life Declarations to remind you of this new way of living.

Use the space on the next page to journal any additional prayers, thoughts, or insights.

# Author's Note

Look at you, amazing Right-Now Woman! You made it to the end of this study. Well done! I celebrate you, and I am incredibly proud of you.

You aren't the same woman you were before beginning this twenty-eight-day adventure. You knew there had to be more to life than how you were living. Hence, you bravely chose to step out into unfamiliar territory, willing to learn this new way of undistracted living. You allowed God to take you by the hand, to guide you, teach you, and grow you into the Right-Now Woman you are today.

I know this wasn't easy. At times you faced uncomfortable realities, you opened yourself up to new possibilities, and you kept putting one foot in front of the other, receiving all God had for you. Your relationship with Him has grown, and you now have a bigger picture of His wonderful plans and purposes for your life—even if they aren't quite clear yet. You are now equipped—through God's grace and power—to live the abundant life Jesus came to give you.

It doesn't end here, however. This is just the beginning of the greatest adventure of your life. On this side of heaven, the distractions will still appear. You likely won't overcome them perfectly, but you are now prepared and able to thrive in living a beautiful, undistracted life. As you do so, others will naturally be drawn to you. Inviting them on this adventure with you will make it even more enjoyable.

I wish I could give you a big hug or high five right now. Until the day I can, continue to remember this: you are a Right-Now Woman because right now matters.

# Notes

1     Harvard University. "Wandering Mind Not a Happy Mind." The Harvard Gazette, accessed July 20, 2022. https://news.harvard.edu/gazette/story/2010/11/wandering-mind-not-a-happy-mind/.

# Appendix

**Access the free printable** of *Lord, Help Me Be a Blessing Today* referenced in Day 24 and found Chapter 12 of *Right Now Matters* at julielefebure.com/resources.

**Find the free printable** of the Right Now Matters Scripture and Prayer Cards referenced in Day 26 and found in Chapter 13 of *Right Now Matters* at rightnowmatters.com.

**Access the printable** of the Right-Now Women Life Declarations referenced in Day 28 and found in Chapter 14 of *Right Now Matters* at rightnowmatters.com.

# Answer Key

## DAY 3

Word search answers

| A | S | F | R | I | E | N | D | S | E | T | R | O | X | P |
|---|---|---|---|---|---|---|---|---|---|---|---|---|---|---|
| E | L | A | S | T | I | N | G | A | U | C | Z | V | Q | L |
| P | G | E | H | H | K | N | W | V | D | S | A | E | A | G |
| O | B | K | R | T | G | R | D | O | U | X | E | R | Q | E |
| H | E | A | R | T | Y | U | G | R | N | B | V | J | G | N |
| B | N | W | M | O | W | E | A | Q | D | A | X | O | C | C |
| X | L | A | P | G | L | V | P | L | I | V | E | Y | V | O |
| Z | Y | E | N | U | F | O | C | U | S | B | N | E | M | U |
| G | N | I | S | S | E | L | B | T | T | C | F | D | T | R |
| Y | I | T | N | E | S | E | R | P | R | U | A | I | C | A |
| T | D | F | G | H | J | L | A | K | A | O | M | P | A | G |
| O | F | S | T | I | M | E | V | J | C | H | I | N | P | E |
| D | E | V | B | M | O | M | E | N | T | E | L | I | M | S |
| A | T | R | I | N | S | P | I | R | E | I | Y | P | U | L |
| Y | Q | D | S | A | A | B | U | N | D | A | N | J | K |   |

## DAY 27

Scrambled word answers

loved
chosen
handiwork
redeemed
forgiven
blameless
holy
set free
new creation
temple
child of God
wonderfully made
God's image

# About the Author

Julie Lefebure is the author of *Right Now Matters: Empowering Right-Now Women in a Culture of Distraction.* She is also the host of the *Encouragement for Real Life Podcast.* There she offers hope, inspiration, and encouragement based on biblical principles to help women live the abundant lives Jesus came to give them. Julie speaks at various women's events and groups, and she is the founder, host, and presenter of a local quarterly women's event, "Real Encouragement *LIVE!*"

Julie lives in rural Iowa, is an avid tandem bicyclist with her husband, and enjoys outdoor dining, hanging out with her family, and sunrises and sunsets. Find Julie at julielefebure.com and @julielefebure.